THE
FOOD COMBINER'S
MEAL PLANNER

D1439873

About the Author

Kathryn Marsden is the author of the bestseller *The Food Combining Diet* and of the equally successful *Food Combining In 30 Days* and *Kathryn Marsden's Super Skin*.

She is a qualified nutritionist and also holds a Diploma in Clinical Nutrition and Nutritional Counselling. She is a Member of the Faculty of the Tisserand Institute, of the Society of Nutritional Counsellors, the Register of Nutritional Therapists and of the British Natural Hygiene Society. Her lectures on health and beauty and stress management are in demand all over the world.

Kathryn contributes to some of the best known women's magazines and the health press and, for the last three years, has written a monthly nutrition column for *New Woman* magazine. She broadcasts regularly on BBC and independent radio and is well known for her television work. She has returned recently from another superbly successful media tour of Australia and the Far East, with TV appearances in Sydney, Brisbane, Melbourne, Tasmania, Singapore and Malaysia.

Apart from travelling and writing, Kathryn particularly enjoys gardening, reading, walking, tuneful music and looking after her husband and rescued cats.

THE FOOD COMBINER'S MEAL PLANNER

KATHRYN MARSDEN

Thorsons
An Imprint of HarperCollinsPublishers

Thorsons
An Imprint of HarperCollins*Publishers*
77–85 Fulham Palace Road
Hammersmith, London W6 8JB

First published by Thorsons 1994
9 7 5 3   4 6 8 10

© Kathryn Marsden 1994

Kathryn Marsden asserts the moral right to
be identified as the author of this work

A catalogue record for this book
is available from the British Library

ISBN 0 7225 2915 5

Typeset by Harper Phototypesetters Limited,
Northampton, England
Printed in Great Britain by
HarperCollinsManufacturing Glasgow

All rights reserved. No part of this publication may be
reproduced, stored in a retrieval system, or transmitted,
in any form or by any means, electronic, mechanical,
photocopying, recording or otherwise, without the prior
permission of the publishers.

Contents

❧

Acknowledgments

———— ∾ ————

The Chinese do not draw any distinction between food and medicine.

Lin Yutang, The Importance of Living

There can be few books in existence that are born from the efforts of only one person, the author. *The Food Combiner's Meal Planner* would never have seen the light of day without the considerable support and assistance that I have received from friends and colleagues around the world. I have cause to be grateful to many generous people and this is my opportunity to express not only my appreciation but also my admiration for their extensive knowledge and forbearance. You are all special; I am fortunate indeed:

Jean Joice — a particular thank you for her most valuable input and meticulous proofreading.

Doris Grant, for her cheer and encouragement.

Stuart MacDonald, Sydney, Australia.

Gill McPhee, Sydney, Australia.

Alice at the Australia Institute of Aboriginal Studies, Canberra, Australia.

Rodney Brennan, Principal, Nature Care College of Naturopathic and Traditional Medicine, Artamon, New South Wales.

Blackmores, Australia and UK.

Megan Slyfield and Sarah Sutton.

Dr John Stirling, who helps so much with the checking of the technical detail in my manuscripts and his wife Sharon for never complaining about the time it all takes.

Penny Woolley for her thoughtfulness and constancy.

My husband, Ralph Marsden, for changing the direction of my life so much for the better and for never once whingeing about the mountains of work I throw at him!

And to my friends and colleagues in Singapore to whom this book is especially dedicated:

Leow Swee Kheng.

Prasanna Nair, Joachin Tan and Thomas Tay at i.MAGE PR.

Kwan Yew Huat, Boey Poh Geok and Alicia Chong of Inchcape Healthcare, Singapore.

For their kindness, courtesy and hospitality.

Preface

> An amazing number of food allergies clear up completely when supposedly allergic individuals learn to eat their foods in digestible combinations. What they suffer from is not allergy . . . but indigestion.
>
> *Dr Herbert M. Shelton*

Food combining has fascinated me for years – and I'm not alone. Interest in this wonderful way of eating is not confined to the United Kingdom and the United States but is now worldwide. As I discovered during a recent working tour of Australia and the Far East, food combining is as international as food itself. Those who teach and write on the subject and the many thousands of others who now follow food combining, emanate from many countries and speak many different languages.

Whilst the basic principle of food combining is sacrosanct (i.e. not mixing proteins and starches at the same meal), almost everyone will have a slightly different way of achieving the same formula. This is not surprising since there have been several celebrated food combining masters who, over the years, have approached the science of food combining from a variety of viewpoints.

When I first began *my* research into food combining, I found that these contradictions, although only minor, meant that every volume varied in the way it sorted and arranged its food lists; a source of potential confusion, especially for those new to the concept. The answer, I realized, was to create an all-encompassing directory which could be used by anyone, meat-eater or vegetarian, in any country, of any nationality.

The Food Combiner's Meal Planner is a kind of *super-index*, a comprehensive categorization of foods, which is designed as a companion to other food combining titles. An ideal shopping or kitchen guide, it will tell you at a glance which foods combine successfully and which do not. I hope, also, that it answers some of the most common food combining questions.

The Food Combiner's Meal Planner makes no attempt to support or criticize any particular writer's view, only to complement and clarify; also to clear up any confusion which may have arisen due to inevitable past oversights or omissions.

We all know the old adage about never judging a book by its cover. The research for *The Food Combiner's Meal Planner* has convinced me that one should never judge a book by its size, either! I almost disappeared behind the mountains of tables, encyclopaedias and other tomes of reference. Compiling these lists has been an education in itself and an indication of just how many fascinating foods there are available around the world.

The variety of items which are eaten by the many

peoples of this planet is truly remarkable. When you begin to dip into the *Meal Planner*, you will — inevitably — find some unusual foods, some which you have never eaten, or in some cases, not heard of until today.

One of the *advantages* of the incredible improvements in communications and transport systems is that more places than ever are able to export and import produce to and from other countries. Some foods which only a few years ago would have been familiar to just one particular area can now be purchased worldwide.

Working on *The Food Combiner's Meal Planner* has been a fascinating experience — and enormous fun. I hope you find it useful and enjoyable.

Kathryn Marsden
Wiltshire, England
January 1994

Author's Note

The information Kathryn includes in her books has been accumulated from her own personal research and experience which, from the feedback she has received, would appear to have helped many people. However, these guidelines are not intended to be prescriptive, nor are they an attempt to diagnose or treat any particular condition. If you are concerned in any way about your health, Kathryn recommends that you consult your own medical adviser without delay.

It is wise to keep your GP informed of the progress of any symptoms, of any dietary changes and of any supplement programme you decide to follow. Obtain as many details about your condition from your medical adviser as you can — and ask plenty of questions about any medicines which may be recommended — but do not stop taking any existing prescribed medication without first consulting your doctor. Follow a sensible diet which contains a wide variety of fresh, unprocessed foods, take regular exercise and avoid cigarette smoke.

Kathryn is always delighted to hear from readers but regrets that, due to an ever-increasing workload, she can no longer reply to every letter received. She is unable to comment on individual cases unless accompanied by a doctor's letter of referral and a full medical/health history.

What is Food Combining?

If you have read — and I don't know why you
should but it will make it very awkward for me
if you haven't — two books called *The Food
Combining Diet* and *Food Combining In 30 Days*,
then you will need no introduction to this one.

*With deference to A.A. Milne's
'The Hums of Pooh' (1929)*

Successful food combining is based on the simple
principle of not mixing proteins and starches at the
same meal. It works by improving the digestion, sorting
out the clutter which has stockpiled in the intestines,
eliminating accumulated poisons, improving energy
levels, balancing weight and generally enhancing health
and well-being.

If you're already familiar with food combining, you'll
also probably have heard it called 'Haying' or 'the Hay
way', after Dr William Howard Hay. But, contrary to
common belief, Dr Hay did not invent the now famous
diet which so often bears his name, nor did he claim
that he had.

The history of food combining goes back at least two
thousand years, having been followed by the Essene

sect in Palestine. Serious research was started in the 1850s by a group of doctors, called natural hygienists, who discovered that digestion and absorption of nutrients could be seriously impaired if foods were eaten in incongruous combinations *at the same meal*. The work of famous American hygienists Drs Russell Trall and J.H. Tilden substantiated these earlier findings that, when the body does not digest food properly, it can become toxic and that toxicity leads to disease. Dr Hay, who wrote several books and articles during the 1920s and '30s, was a disciple of Dr Tilden, although Hay developed his own ideas in a slightly different direction. Food combining has surfaced again recently in other works such as Leslie Kenton's *Biogenic Diet*, the Walb system in Germany, Frenchman Michel Montignac's *Dine Out and Lose Weight* and *Fit for Life* by Harvey and Marilyn Diamond.

However, probably the most exciting research was carried out by Dr Herbert S. Shelton, generally considered by practitioners to be the guru of natural hygiene and food combining philosophy. From 1928 to 1981, Dr Shelton operated a training college and clinic in San Antonio, Texas, where he compiled the most comprehensive data on the proper combination of foods so far available. His work continues there, carried out by medically qualified staff. The amazing extent of Shelton's work (and the abundance of other writings on the subject) makes an absolute nonsense of the oft-quoted but completely erroneous criticism that there is no scientific evidence to support the use of food combining!

Eating Healthily and Well

Food combining is all about healthy eating for a healthy life. If the disappointing results of so many dietary surveys and population studies are anything to go by, it's likely that more people would benefit from taking a closer look at food combining fare. Sad to say, research continues to suggest that healthy eating habits are rare indeed. But how many of us really know what constitutes a 'properly balanced diet' or have the time or the inclination to prepare one?

Enhanced Energy and Well-being

Becoming a food combiner means that meal planning is suddenly much easier. By following a few simple guidelines, you can achieve — with ease — that elusive 'balance', enjoying just the right amounts of fresh fruits, vegetables and dietary fibre and a sensible (and healthy) intake of fats and oils. Food combining helps not just towards better health and enhanced well-being but also to a balanced weight and increased energy.

Easy to Follow

Whether you have long experience of food combining or are a newcomer to the art, *The Food Combiner's Meal Planner* has been created to help you select the right foods, at a glance and without fuss. This neat little pocket book lists hundreds of foods from all around the world in their correct categories and is an essential companion to other food combining titles. If you want to know whether a food is alkaline-forming, if it's classed as protein or starch, or to find out the best way to combine certain foods, then *The Food Combiner's Meal Planner* is for you.

Choosing a 'new' food each day — or even each week — will also widen your eating horizons, bringing a huge variety of fresh food ideas to your shopping basket and kitchen stores. Whatever your nationality and whether you are meat-eating or vegetarian, *The Food Combiner's Meal Planner* is here to help you.

Why Do We Need to Combine Foods More Carefully?

It should come really as no surprise that eating habits in the developed, supposedly wealthy nations of the world are far from healthy. The motley mixture which many of us eat each day could be likened to an untidy, bulging and never-cleaned-out cupboard — full of unnecessary and unidentifiable junk. Complicate the diet with inappropriate food combinations and our digestive systems have considerable difficulty sorting out the muddle. As Dr Jonn Matsen explains so graphically in his wonderful book *Eating Alive*, 'we expect our system to somehow magically grind it all up, sort it out, use the good, eliminate the bad, all without any noise or complaint'.

When foods are not broken down properly, health-giving nutrients may be only partially absorbed or missed out on altogether. That consequent lack of nourishment can lead, all too often, to lack of energy, lethargy, weight problems and ill health.

Most people are familiar with the digestive 'traffic jam'. Food seems to lie heavily on the stomach, the heartburn burns, the abdomen bloats, the bowels misbehave and trapped wind can cause pain and, sometimes, embarrassment. *Long-term, poor digestion can play havoc not only with how fit you are but how fat you become.* It's not always overeating and under-exercising which cause weight problems, but the inadequate consumption or absorption of the right kind of nourishment.

Experience in practice shows that one of the major causes of all this distress is the mixing of protein foods and starch foods together at the same sitting; Drs Hay and Shelton and other food combining researchers believe that different food groups need not only varying lengths of time to be digested, but also different conditions. When several incompatible food types are consumed at the same meal, the body takes far longer to deal with the mad mixture, drawing on valuable energy reserves which are often already in short supply. Unpleasant things can happen to food that lies around in the system for too long; it putrefies, goes off, produces gas – well, you get the picture. Speed up the 'transit time' of food, enhance digestion and improve absorption – and such symptoms can be a thing of the past.

So, let's look at food combining categories in a little more detail.

What is a Starch?

For the purposes of food combining, starches include all the grains such as oats, rice and rye and all the foods made from them, i.e cereals, flour, biscuits, bread etc. In other words, each of these foods contains a *concentrated* level of starch. A few vegetables which contain large amounts of starch (potatoes, sweet potatoes, yams, sweetcorn and so on) are also found in this category. You'll find a full list of Grains and Cereals from page 146 and the Starchy Vegetables from page 159. Throughout the reference tables in *The Food Combiner's Meal Planner*, starch foods are marked with an 'S'.

Try to make one main meal per day a starch-based meal and remember that starchy foods mix well with all kinds of starchy vegetables, and with non-starchy vegetables and salads which are listed from page 116. Seeds and herbs (pages 132 and 128) are also excellent accompaniments to starch meals.

What is a Protein?

Proteins are those foods which contain *concentrated* levels of protein such as meat, poultry, cheese, eggs, fish, yoghurt etc. Try to make one meal per day a protein-based meal and remember that proteins combine happily with the 'mix-with-anything' vegetables and salads listed from page 116. Seeds and herbs (pages 132 and 128) go well with protein meals too. Throughout the reference lists, proteins are marked with a 'P'.

What is a 'Mix-With-Anything' Food?

Think of the 'mix-with-anything' foods as impartial or unbiased — foods that are neither *concentrated* proteins nor *concentrated* starches and so will mix happily with anything. Salads, seeds, herbs, spices, fats and oils and non-starchy vegetables are good companions to either proteins or starches. Check out the Quick Reference Chart on page 167 to see how the mix-with-anything foods (in the centre column) fit into food combining. Throughout the reference tables, 'mix-with-anything' foods are marked 'M'.

(In some earlier food combining books these mix-with-anything foods were termed 'Neutral' – a term which I no longer use, as it has led to confusion in the past. For example, foods which are neither acid-forming nor alkaline-forming [see below] have also been referred to as 'Neutral' in some food combining books.)

Try to mix your protein-based meal and your starch-based meal each day with non-starchy vegetables or salads. Generous quantities of fresh vegetables or salad foods should form part of all your main meals.

What Does Alkaline-Forming and Acid-Forming Mean?

In 'food combining speak', we often hear the words acid and alkaline, but what are they all about? When we digest our food, the metabolic 'leftovers' include different kinds of mineral deposits which are needed in the right amounts to maintain good health.

Alkaline-forming foods are as follows:

- Fresh fruits
- All vegetables (whether they are starchy or non-

starchy doesn't matter) *except for acid-forming asparagus*
- Salad foods
- Herbs
- Seeds
- Almond and Brazil nuts (the only alkaline-forming nuts)
- Millet (the only alkaline-forming grain)

Acid-forming foods include nearly all the proteins and starches.

In order to get the balance right, the great majority of us need to create more of the minerals which come from alkaline-forming fresh produce and fewer of the acid-forming kind. It therefore makes sense to increase our intake of vegetables, fruits, salads and herbs and cut down a little on those protein and starch foods which we tend to eat too many of anyway. This does not, however, mean that we should *give up* protein or starch — far from it! Food combining balances your intake automatically if you follow the '*one protein, one starch and one alkaline meal per day*' rule (see below).

Or put another way:

Remember that food combining achieves the 'just right' level of alkaline-forming and acid-forming foods if you have:

One protein-based meal with vegetables or salad
One starch-based meal with vegetables or salad
    and
One salad, vegetable or fruit meal which does not include *concentrated* protein or starch (in other words, one alkaline-forming meal)

If you do find it a little difficult to stick to one protein, one starch and one alkaline-forming meal per day (if meals are being prepared for you by someone else, for example), then compromise by aiming for seven protein meals, seven starch meals and seven alkaline meals each week.

Food Combining In 30 Days and *The Food Combining Diet* give more information on the importance of alkaline/acid balance for good health.

Throughout the book, acid-forming foods are marked with a minus sign ('-') and alkaline-forming foods are marked with a plus sign ('+'). If they are neither acid-forming nor alkaline-forming, they'll be marked with 'n'.

No Need to 'Give Up and Suffer'!

Food combining doesn't mean reducing your intake or giving up pasta, poultry, prawns, plaice or any of the acid-forming foods which you particularly enjoy. They are still good for you. Nor does learning how to combine them properly make meals any the less delicious. It does, however, mean that valuable nutrients are properly dealt with by the digestive system (perhaps for the first time in years!), thereby enhancing and improving your health.

Tried and Tested Success

I have been using food combining methods in my nutrition practice for many years and never cease to be amazed at the health-enhancing powers of what are, in fact, the simplest of dietary changes. For me, there is no doubt that food combining works! *The Food Combiner's Meal Planner* was really born out of my own personal need for a comprehensive listing of international foods. Wherever you live, whatever your lifestyle and whichever your favourite food combining book, this pocket reference will enable you to combine your meals with renewed interest and energy.

How to Use this Book

Animals in nature don't combine their foods improperly. That is the beauty of it. They eat one food at a time.

Harvey Diamond

Before you begin to use any of the tables, I would recommend reading the introductory chapters on pages 20 to 38 and, also, familiarizing yourself with the two basic and most important food combining rules:

- Avoid mixing proteins with starches at the same meal
- Avoid mixing fruit or fruit juices with proteins or starches (see page 20)

And take things easy. 'By the inch, it's a cinch, by the yard, it's hard' goes the old adage; so don't push yourself too far too quickly. Remember that any beneficial changes, however small, are going to be for the better. Introducing too many changes at one time can put strain on an already exhausted or undernourished system.

Don't feel pressured. Begin by food combining for one day each week, for two days in the second week, three in the third and so on. Or follow the step-by-step guide in my new health plan, *Food Combining In 30 Days* (see Recommended Reading).

Far from restricting your intake, you'll soon see that *The Food Combiner's Meal Planner* gives you the opportunity to enjoy a greater variety of foodstuffs than ever before as well as almost endless and exciting food combinations. By turning to the A–Z of Foods which begins on page 39, you can check, at a glance, the group to which a food belongs. In addition, find out if it is a *protein*, a *starch*, whether it's *alkaline-* or *acid-forming*, if it's a food that combines well or one that should be avoided or eaten only occasionally. Is it categorized as fruit, fish, spice, seed, pulse or pasta? The 'Family' column in the A–Z of Foods will guide you to the relevant 'Food Families' listing from page 39 onwards.

What the Symbols Mean

The plus '+' indicates that the food is alkaline-forming and the minus '-' that it is acid-forming. (The terms 'acid' and 'alkali' are explained on page 7.)

An 'n' means that a food is neither acid-forming nor alkaline-forming.

'P' means protein, which you can read more about on page 6. Protein foods are listed on pages 136, 139 etc.

'S' stands for starch. Read more about this group on page 5. Starch foods are listed on pages 146, 159 etc.

'M' means 'Mixes-with-anything' – in other words, foods which are neither concentrated proteins nor concentrated starches and which can be included at a protein meal or a starch meal. Page 6 explains all about these versatile mixable foods.

Foods marked 'O' (for example, fresh fruits and fruit juices) prefer to be eaten on their own, i.e. separately from proteins and starches (see page 20 for further information).

Foods marked with an asterisk '*' are those which, preferably, should not be taken in large quantities.

Some entries are listed as 'Foods to Avoid' and these foods should, indeed, be avoided if at all possible. Pages 29–32 give more information on the not-so-healthy foods. It's important to be familiar with this group before you begin to food combine.

For an easy reference guide to symbols, see the box on page 38.

Food Families

The Food Combiner's Meal Planner also classifies foods according to their 'families'; for example, Meat, Poultry and Game under one heading, Grains and Cereals under another, Non-Starchy Vegetables under another and so on. This section uses the same symbols as in the A–Z of Foods.

EXAMPLE 1:

Say that you are unsure how cream fits into food combining. It's made from milk but has a high fat content. So is it a protein or a fat?

Here's what to do:

Turn to the A–Z of Foods on page 39 and under the letter 'C', you will find cream. Look along the line and it will tell you that cream can be found under 'Fats and Oils'. Turn to this section in the Food Families list on page 154 and you'll see that cream is classed as a fat. The letter 'M' indicates that it can be mixed with any other food, but the asterisk '*' means it should be eaten in moderation only.

EXAMPLE 2:

You know that yoghurt is a protein food but want to find out if it's acid- or alkaline-forming. The A–Z of Foods will tell you that yoghurt is marked with a '+' which means alkaline-forming. Or, you could obtain the same information by turning immediately to 'Eggs and Dairy Products' in the Food Families list.

EXAMPLE 3:

Suppose you want to check up on where sweetcorn fits into food combining. Under 'S' in the A–Z of Foods you'll see sweetcorn categorized as a 'Starchy Vegetable' (sveg). As a starchy vegetable, then, sweetcorn will mix with any Non-Starchy Vegetables or Salads as well as, in small amounts, with other starches – but not with protein foods.

EXAMPLE 4:

You fancy an apple with your snack lunch. Under 'A' in the A–Z of Foods, apples are classed, not surprisingly, with fruits, which prefer not to be mixed with other foods. But this doesn't mean the apple is banned – just enjoy it *before* your sandwich instead of afterwards. 'Turn to page 20 for more information on this.

Worldwide Choices

The Food Combiner's Meal Planner will help you to make the most of the enormous variety of foods now available. The book is sold in many different countries and serves a wide range of different cuisines and cultures. Some food names may therefore seem unfamiliar in just the same way that your most common foods may be a complete mystery to someone else in another country. However, the growing accessibility of fresh produce from other parts of the world means that more and more of us can widen the scope of our food choices by sampling a whole range of new dishes. If your particular preference does not appear to be available in the local grocery store or supermarket, then branch out into health food shops, delicatessens and those which specialize in ethnic cuisine. For example, an Indian or Chinese food market can be a veritable 'Aladdin's Cave' of delicacies.

Naming Names

There are many instances where the same food may be known by different names in different parts of the world. For example, the cactus fruit is also called 'prickly pear', the macadamia nut is the 'Queensland nut' and cos lettuce, 'romaine'. Where alternative names apply, they will both appear in the A–Z of Foods. The most commonly used name is the one which will appear in the 'Food Families' listing. Cactus fruit can be found under the letter 'C', prickly pear under 'P' and so on. Where a particular food is also well known by its Chinese name, then that will appear in brackets after the English designation.

Hassle-Free Healthy Eating

As an added bonus, *The Food Combiner's Meal Planner* will make balancing the nutrients in your diet far easier. For example, following the food combining rules means that you will increase your intake of those all-important alkaline-forming vegetables, salads and fresh fruit, reduce your intake of refined and manufactured foods, take on board the right kind of fats and the recommended amounts of protein foods and cereal fibre — all without having to think about it. Food combining works it out for you. To guide you, it's worth repeating the all-important daily aims of:

One protein-based meal with vegetables or salad
One starch-based meal with vegetables or salad
    and
One alkaline-forming meal of just fruit, vegetables or
    salad.

Finally, I would recommend that you use *The Food Combiner's Meal Planner* in conjunction with one of the major food combining paperbacks which are available in all good bookstores.

Key	
*	EAT IN MODERATION ONLY
+	ALKALINE-FORMING
–	ACID-FORMING
n	NEITHER acid- nor alkaline-forming
P	PROTEINS
M	MIX-WITH-ANYTHING FOODS
O	EAT SEPARATELY i.e. fruit
S	STARCHES

In the FAMILY column:

sveg	starchy vegetable
nsveg	non-starchy vegetable

Important Note

Where there has, in the past, been a discrepancy or disparity over a particular food (i.e. one book puts something in one category and another book disagrees), I have gone to the greatest possible lengths to discover which is correct and settle the argument. For example, I came across one food combining book which listed Jerusalem artichoke as a starchy vegetable (well, it does look rather like a potato or taro which are both starchy). On further investigation, I discovered that this type of artichoke contains less starch than a globe artichoke and about the same as that of a leek — both of which are classed as non-starchy vegetables. Further, some books class pumpkin/squash as starch, but the starch levels of fresh pumpkin are less than those for several other non-starchy vegetables including the non-starchy parsnip.

(It is worth bearing in mind that the starch content of vegetables can increase with age and storage. Therefore, an older pumpkin harvested some time ago may be starchy enough to categorise as a starchy vegetable. Use your own judgement when it comes to pumpkins, i.e. very fresh = non-starchy; stored for a longer time = starchy.)

Eggs are generally regarded as *first class protein* and, in all my food-combining books, are treated as *protein* foods. Confusingly, however, some older publications have categorised the egg white as protein but treated the egg yolk as fat. Whilst it's true that egg whites have only tiny traces of fat and egg yolks are rich in fat, a simple calculation reveals that, weight for weight, *egg white and egg yolk contain almost exactly the same amount of PROTEIN each*. This means that *eggs (whether yolks, whites or whole eggs) should be treated as protein*.

Such idiosyncrasies often occur and recur repeatedly due, at worst, to lack of proper investigation and, at best, because of a tendency to ignore the age-old maxim 'Take nobody's word for it'. In other words, mistakes can be copied innocently and with the best of intentions to the point where they are accepted as correct.

What is encouraging is that new information on foods and eating habits is constantly being obtained. In fact, I am grateful to some researchers for pointing out a few long-held but incorrect assumptions of my own about certain areas of food combining. I hope that, in making these small changes, I have not created any further confusion; my aim throughout has been to make *The Food Combiner's Meal Planner* as 'food combiner friendly' as possible and to include the most comprehensive list that available space would allow. If anyone else has gone to the trouble of having certain foods tested in an analytical laboratory but has come up with different results to my own, I would be glad to hear from them. As in any work which takes in as many varied sources of reference, oversights are more than possible. I beg the reader's indulgence and will be most grateful to receive any alternative views and comments.

The Food Combining Fruit Rule

Never under any circumstances eat fruit or fruit salad directly after a meal! You will deprive yourself of its cleansing benefits — and unless your system is totally insensitized after years of dietary abuse — you will probably experience discomfort and indigestion.

Marilyn Diamond

The classic, 'Hay' approach to food combining says that certain fruits and fruit juices can be eaten with protein foods and others with starch foods (see, for example, *Food Combining for Health* by Doris Grant and Jean Joice). If you have been following this method and feel better for it, then fine. Many other teachings (and my own experience in clinical practice) tell us that this may not be such a good idea (see Dr Shelton's work and books by the famous American food combiner Wayne Pickering).

From a purely practical point of view, eating fruit separately can make life simpler. Mixing acidic fruits with protein and very sweet fruits with starch means having to remember not only which *are* which but which *go* with which. It can seem confusing (according to the Hay rule), to be able to combine a just-ripe pear (an acid fruit) with protein, then to find that when it becomes very sweet and ripe, it is compatible only with starch. It can, needless to say, be very hard to judge when that pear crosses the line between one category and another.

But there is an even more important, far simpler, reason for not mixing fruits with other foods. Fruit travels very quickly through the stomach (usually 15 to 20 minutes) and juices at even greater speed. If hindered by slower moving foods (i.e. proteins or starches), the fruit will be 'held up' and begin to ferment. Fermentation causes a build-up of gas and the subsequent pressure causes pain. Eat it on its own and not only will the fruit be able to move on to the next stage of digestion without delay but the nutrients it contains will be absorbed far more efficiently.

In my experience with patients, one of the commonest causes of indigestion is fruit — but not when it is eaten separately on an empty stomach. Problems are more likely to occur when fruit is shoved down the tubes in hot pursuit of a hastily grabbed sandwich or as a dessert after a main meal. One of my patients likes to tell me that the grumbling noise he used to experience in his stomach was the fruit 'arguing' with the food he used to mix with it. Now that he eats fruit separately, the grumbling noises — and years of heartburn — have ceased.

The 'keep fruit separate' rule features in my books *Food Combining In 30 Days* and *The Food Combining Diet*, and in books by Harvey and Marilyn Diamond, Leslie Kenton, Wayne Pickering and Dr Shelton himself (see Recommended Reading for more details).

If you follow Dr Hay's personal rules, you'll find that acid fruits are allowed with protein foods and very sweet, starchy fruits are allowed with starch foods. However, my in-depth studies of other writers and my own personal research into food combining, backed up by experience in practice, has reinforced my long-held view that proteins and starches are antagonistic towards fruit.

However, this does not mean that there is necessarily a *right* or *wrong* way, just differing opinions. Lots of people have followed Hay's rules for many years and found them more than adequate, indeed some exceptional results have been achieved. Devotees of the indomitable Doris Grant and delightful Jean Joice — who are loyal to Dr Hay's methods — find their recommendations most beneficial. Others say that the Shelton, Diamond or Marsden systems are simpler to understand and operate. Whichever route you decide to follow, if you feel happy with it, then that method is probably the best one for you. In any event, *The Food Combiner's Meal Planner* should fit in with your favourites.

For the benefit of those who find that eating fruit with or after a meal causes them discomfort, then this is the fruit rule which I have found to be of the greatest benefit and which I always recommend to my own patients:

Avoid mixing fruit with other food and especially not with proteins or starches. Always eat fruit on an empty stomach either before a meal, as a between-meal snack or as a fruit-only meal on its own.

You may also find the following tips useful:

- Queries sometimes arise when a fruit also falls into the vegetable camp. For example, avocado is strictly a fruit but is used more widely as a salad vegetable. For food combining purposes, treat avocado as an alkaline-forming vegetable.
- Tomatoes are fruits but are used also in savoury dishes and treated as vegetables in some countries. Raw tomatoes can be mixed with anything but become very acidic (and potentially indigestible) once cooked. So the answer here is to avoid cooked tomatoes wherever possible. Ripe, skinned, pulped, raw tomatoes make good substitutes.
- Where a vegetable is sometimes used in sweet dishes, for example, pumpkin/squash, then it will still be classed in its original vegetable category as a mix-with-anything item.
- Canned and stewed fruits can be useful emergency stand-bys but, all food combining writers agree, should not be consumed in large quantities. Once cooked or heat treated, they no longer contain the same nourishment as the fresh version, losing much of their valuable vitamin content and can be much more difficult to digest.
- Dried fruits, like fresh, are all alkaline-forming and mix well with each other, but should not be combined with starches or proteins. Avoid buying dried fruit that has been sprayed with shiny glazing agent or preservative — choose additive-free products from health-food stores, store in a cool place and eat before the sell-by date.
- Some experts suggest that sweet fruits should not

be combined with acidic ones. Actually, I have not found this to be a problem except in the case of plums and rhubarb (which are extremely acidic and, therefore, best avoided altogether) and melons (a nourishing but special case — see below). Rhubarb is, in fact, classified as a vegetable stem but should still be avoided. In my experience, it is when fruits are mixed with proteins or starches that disagreeable noises and noxious gases begin to emanate from the digestive system! The answer here is to use common sense. If you have found that combining certain fruits together gives you grief, then avoid those combinations. However, for most people, fruits mix happily with each other in fruit salads or compotes as long as they are *not* accompanied by proteins or starches.

- Nutritious melons travel through the system at break-neck speed. As a result, I like to call them the Greta Garbo of fruits since they are best eaten entirely alone. In other words, try to avoid mixing them with anything at all, not even with other fruits.

- Adding small amounts of fresh fruit to bio-yoghurt, does not usually cause digestive disasters, simply because yoghurt itself is easy to digest and has a faster transit time than heavier proteins.

The Last Word on Pulses

Legumes are potent medicine ...
Jean Carper, The Food Pharmacy

If there is one area of food combining confusion, it lies with the pulses or legumes. Those new to food combining — and also those who doubt its benefits — often ask, if the protein/starch rule really matters, how Mother Nature would explain the existence of pulses, which are a natural mixture of proteins and starches.

Well, we hear a lot about how pulses provide valuable proteins for those who don't eat meat — which indeed is true but, in fact, nearly all pulses are basically *starchy*, containing more starch than protein. It is clear, therefore, that they would not combine well with concentrated proteins such as meat, poultry, eggs or cheese. In some traditional dishes, it is common for pulses to be mixed with grains — legumes and rice, for example — which is clearly better from the food combining point of view.

Essentially, then, pulses should be treated as starches and can be mixed with other starches *in moderation*, as well as with salads and non-starchy vegetables.

There is just one exception: soya beans. These also contain a mix of both protein and starch but the other way around — in other words, more protein than starch. Soya beans, then, should never be combined with starches.

An added complication is the notorious reputation of pulses for creating discomfort. As a result, some food combining writers do not recommend them at all. However, this view seems to me to be unnecessarily pedantic. Pulses are an excellent source of nourishment for everyone and especially for vegans and vegetarians who do not eat flesh foods. In addition, beans — whether they are black-eyed, white, navy, red, split or soya — have the capacity to reduce cholesterol, balance blood glucose, lower blood pressure, inhibit certain types of cancer and improve immeasurably the functions of the bowel. Rather a lot of benefits to give up, I'd say.

It is true that pulses are infamous for causing bloating and flatulence but their indigestibility is usually the result of either:

incorrect combination with other foods *or*
inadequate or faulty preparation.

So which is the right way to eat them?

Enjoy Your Pulses!

Remember the following rules to combine pulses happily and avoid indigestibility:

- Pulses mix well with all the non-starchy vegetables and the salad foods.
- They never combine well with proteins.
- They prefer not to be mixed with starches except in small amounts.
- If you mix them with grains such as quinoa, millet or rice, then do so in moderation; in other words, not every day and not in large quantities.
- Soya products are treated differently from other pulses since soya beans are protein foods. They should never be mixed with starches. All soya products are acid-forming except *beancurd/tofu* and *dow see/salted black beans* which, because they have been through a fermentation process, are rendered alkaline-forming and easier to digest.
- Once sprouted, pulses become non-starchy, alkaline-forming foods which can be combined comfortably with anything!
- Fresh garden peas and petit pois are classed as non-starchy vegetables since their starch content, at that stage, is minimal. Processed, marrowfat peas, dried peas and pease pudding have a nutrient content closer to other pulses and should therefore be classed as such.
- Prepare pulses properly: after soaking, rinse the pulses several times in fresh water, and when boiling them scoop off any white scum on the surface of the water. If using canned beans, rinse before use.
- Always chew pulses thoroughly in order to help break down the starchy molecules which are responsible for producing gas and indigestion.

A full list of pulses appears from page 155. Soya beans and other soya products are on page 158. My book *The Food Combining Diet* contains more information on pulses and how to prepare them.

Not-So-Healthy Foods

———— ❧ ————

> Whole foods are simply fresh, natural, edible
> things as close to their natural state as possible
> . . . . Partial or fragmented foods are often called
> 'refined' as if stripping foods of some of their
> coarser elements makes them more worthy of
> attention and respect.
>
> *Annemarie Colbin*, Food and Healing

Foods to Avoid

Food combining is not just about choosing the right combinations, it's also about healthy eating and renewed vitality. I am always dismayed by health writers who lay down unbending, uncompromising rules and pepper their text with negative instructions such as 'never' and 'don't'. Most nutritional 'rules' are made of rubber, in other words, they can bend without being broken. This applies particularly to food combining. If eaten every day or in large quantities, however, the foods in the list below are likely to hinder, rather than help you towards better health — which is why the majority of them do not appear in the A–Z of Foods on pages 39 to 103.

When foods are highly refined, loaded with fat, sugar or additives, they go against our usual view of what is healthy to eat. And when concentrated protein and starch turn up in the same product, they clearly do not fit into food combining philosophy. In addition, some of the items listed here still have unresolved question marks hanging over their long-term safety; for example, beef because of the problems in some countries with BSE; margarine and the concerns over hydrogenated oils; artificial additives and the increased risk of allergic reactions. And, if all that were not enough, nearly all these not-so-healthy foods are acid-forming, too; an abundance of them is bound to disturb the body's delicate alkaline/acid balance. Whilst small amounts — or occasional treats — are hardly likely to cause problems, it is wise in my view to cut right down on the following items:

Sweets
Chocolate
Cocoa Powder
White or Brown Sugar
Glucose Powder
Treacle
Golden Syrup
Sugary Foods
Jelly (Jello)
Artificial Sweeteners
Artificial Preservatives, Flavours and Colours
Sugar-Laden Jam and Marmalade
Cornflour, Refined White Flour and all Products Containing it
Shop-Bought Cakes and Sweet Biscuits

Shop-Bought Pies and Pastries

Processed White Bread

Deep-Fried and Fatty Foods

Factory-Farmed, Non-Organic, Beef and Beef Products

Meat Pasties

Steak and Kidney Pie

Chicken Pie

Haggis

Faggots

Pork and Pork Products — Including Ham, Bacon, Sausages, Pig's Liver and Pork Pies (although if you can find organic, free-range pork this can be eaten in moderation)

Cow's Milk (can cause digestive difficulties, especially when mixed with other foods; if you wish to increase your calcium intake, eat plain live yoghurt)

Instant Coffee

Strong Tea

Cola and Other Sweet Carbonated Drinks, Squashes and Pasteurized/Packaged Orange Juice

Burned, Browned, Seared, Barbecued or Spicy Food (there is some evidence that excessive intake of these foods can increase the risk of certain digestive cancers, although small quantities are unlikely to be harmful)

Beers and Spirits

MSG (Monosodium Glutamate)

Malt vinegar

Yeast extract (can be very troublesome for anyone suffering from Candida albicans, or yeast overgrowth; see *The Food Combining Diet*)

Salty Foods and Pre-Salted Snacks, Including Peanuts and Crisps

Packaged and Tinned Convenience Foods

Ready Meals and Prepackaged 'T.V.' Dinners

All Tinned and Preserved Meats

Take-Away Pizzas, Burgers and Fries

Pizzas with protein toppings (e.g. cheese, salami or anchovies)

Dried Milk and Coffee Creamers

Dried Egg

Ketchup

Rhubarb and Plums (very acidic and difficult to digest so not recommended)

Packet Soups

Battery-Raised Eggs and Battery-Raised Poultry

Processed, Smoked and Coloured Cheese

Smoked Meats and Smoked Fish

Take-Away Sandwiches that have Protein Fillings

Pancakes

Pasta that has Protein Filling or Protein Sauce (e.g. Meat or Cheese)

Fish Pie

Fish in Batter

Hydrogenated Margarines

Foods Containing Hydrogenated Vegetable Oils

Processed, Manufactured Low-Fat Foods

Processed Cooking Oils

Food Combining
Questions and Answers

Scientists, conditioned to wrestling with complex problems, often cannot understand simple concepts nor recognize their importance.
Dr Walter Yellowlees, A Doctor in the Wilderness

Q. *I understand the 'one protein/one starch meal per day' rule but how do I make sure that I eat enough alkaline-forming foods?*

A. That's easy. If you have a small salad or a few vegetables with your protein meal and the same with your starch meal of the day, making the third meal one of fruit only, vegetables only or salad only, then you will achieve the right intake of alkaline-forming foods. Put another way, try to include fresh produce in some form at each meal.

Q. *Most books on food combining say that we should aim for one protein, one starch and one alkaline-forming meal per day. Some health experts also say that protein should be eaten at lunch and others are emphatic about protein evening meals. Does the order really matter?*

A. In my opinion, no. It is purely a matter of personal preference and should also fit in with your personal lifestyle. For example, hypoglycaemics may find it more helpful to eat protein earlier in the day. Those who take regular vigorous exercise may prefer to precede their workout routine with a starch meal (complex carbohydrates); it is wise to leave about an hour before working out — don't exercise on a completely empty stomach. Those who find it difficult to face food first thing in the morning may manage some fresh fruit (which would be the alkaline meal of the day) but might be nauseated by the sight of eggs (protein) or porridge (starch) when they first get up. No, arrange the three meals to suit yourself entirely.

Q. *Some books and articles on health put forward the view that we should eat only local produce when it is in season and that fruits and vegetables not indigenous to our region should be avoided. In* The Food Combiner's Meal Planner, *you suggest that we should eat foods from all over the world. Can you expand on this point?*

A. There is nothing wrong with relying only on fresh local produce; indeed, for some people, this is preferable. My concern is that, especially in those areas which have a less than ideal climate, there is often a minimal choice of local produce available. In the UK, for example, without the benefit of goods from other areas, some stores would be able to provide only a relatively limited selection of fruits and vegetables throughout the winter. Health experts know already that vast numbers of the population are not eating enough fruits and vegetables and are short on a large number of vitamins and minerals. For them, restricting intake further by laying down rules about local, in-season produce is likely to decrease an already inadequate nutrient intake. In addition, faster travel and better transport means that the world gets smaller. A great many people now travel the world on such a regular basis that they would not be in a position to eat only foods local to their own region. I feel that my own health is enhanced by increasing the variety of foods in my diet and by trying out different types of cuisine the world over.

Q. *You say that fruits prefer to be separated from proteins and starches. Should I eat all fruits separately from each other or can I mix them together?*

A. My experience is that nearly all fruits will mix perfectly well together in, say, fruit salads or compotes. It is the mixing of fruits with heavy proteins and starches that appears to cause indigestion and abdominal discomfort. Page 20 gives more information on this.

Q. *Why is it that food combining does not recommend porridge made with milk but allows porridge with cream?*

A. Porridge is, of course, a starchy food so making it with milk (which is a protein) would not be acceptable. However, cream is classed as fat, not protein. Fats and oils are listed as 'mix-with-anything' foods. Cream therefore will combine happily, in moderation, with starch; it certainly makes for delicious porridge!

Q. *How can yoghurt (which is, after all, made from milk)*

*be alkaline-forming when almost all other dairy products are
acid-forming — and is one better than the other?*

A. The action of fermentation which makes the milk
into yoghurt alters the protein structure of the milk,
breaks down the milk sugar (lactose) and improves the
availability of calcium. These alterations to the chemical
composition of pasteurized milk mean that the yoghurt
becomes alkaline-forming. Alkaline-forming yoghurt is
easier to digest than acid-forming milk and the nutrients
from it better absorbed. I would always choose yoghurt
ahead of milk for these reasons.

Q. *How can I continue to food combine properly when I go
out to eat at other people's houses or in restaurants?*

A. If you are eating out, it's actually much simpler than
you might think to continue with your food combining
— there's no need to feel awkward about it.

Chinese, Japanese and Thai food: Much of the better-
quality oriental food now available in restaurants is
lightly cooked — often stir-fried — and uses a wide
selection of delicious and unusual vegetables. I certainly
find it easy to food combine during my business trips to
the Far East. But don't be tempted to choose rice as an
accompaniment to any protein dish. Avoid deep-fried
items and heavily spiced dishes — if in doubt, ask!

French food: Try to avoid choosing anything coated in
a rich sauce, opting instead for lighter dishes. Given the
large selection of meat and fish dishes usually on offer,
you may well decide to make this a protein meal. You
may also be offered a selection of delicious French
cheeses at the end of the meal — so remember to eat this
on its own, not with biscuits.

Italian food: Italian food can be tricky for food combiners: think how often pasta is combined with meat, fish or cheese, and pizzas are generally given protein toppings too. You could try asking for plain pasta with a selection of fresh vegetables – or how about having it just tossed in olive oil, with fresh herbs and freshly ground black pepper? Or you could have a plate of Italian cold meats with a large mixed salad.

Indian food: If you particularly like the rice, naan and pappadums which tend to accompany meat dishes in Indian restaurants, ask for them with a selection of curried vegetables instead of with meat – most Indian restaurants are happy to provide many small dishes of different vegetables for you to try. It's best to avoid the very hot curried dishes!

Middle Eastern food: Lebanese and Turkish restaurants are also adept at providing a variety of small dishes instead of one 'main' course, and this approach can suit food combiners very well; choose, for example, hummus, *fatoush* (fresh vegetables in toasted bread), *falafel* (spicy chick pea balls served with tahini), or *moutabal* (purée of toasted aubergines mixed with garlic and lemon juice).

If you are eating at someone else's house you might be more restricted for choice, but you can quite easily leave the potatoes or rice accompanying a protein dish go without bread or biscuits if you are having cheese.

Overall, unless you eat out every single day, I wouldn't concern yourself too much about restaurant meals. For example, why not food combine carefully for five or six days out of seven, if food combining every day is not possible for you.

AUTHOR'S NOTE

When choosing foods from the following lists, you won't go far wrong if you remember two maxims:

- Proteins and starches are not happy together
- Fruit prefers to be eaten separately from concentrated proteins and starches

Other tips which may help you are as follows:

- Nearly all proteins are acid-forming
- Nearly all starches are acid-forming
- Nearly all vegetables are alkaline-forming
- All fruits are alkaline-forming
- Non-starchy vegetables, salads and herbs mix with anything

Key	
*	EAT IN MODERATION ONLY
+	ALKALINE-FORMING
−	ACID-FORMING
n	NEITHER acid- nor alkaline-forming
P	PROTEINS
M	MIX-WITH-ANYTHING FOODS
O	EAT SEPARATELY i.e. fruit
S	STARCHES
In the FAMILY column:	
sveg	starchy vegetable
nsveg	non-starchy vegetable

Happy food combining!

A–Z of Foods

For beverages see pages 162–163.

* = In moderation only
+ = Alkaline-forming
– = Acid-forming
n = Neither
P = Protein
M = Mix with anything
O = Eat on its own
S = Starch

FOOD	FAMILY	+/-/n	PROTEIN	M/O	STARCH
A					
Aamchur (Amchoor/ Mango Powder)*	spice	–		M	
Abalone	fish	–	P		
Abiu	fruit	+		O	
Acorn Squash	nsveg	+		M	
Adzuki Bean (Aduki)*	pulse	–			
African Horned Melon (Kiwano)	fruit	+		O	
Agar	nsveg	+		M	
Aigwa (Aubergine/Eggplant/ Brinjal)	nsveg	+		M	
Ajwain*	spice	–		M	
Albumen	eggs/ dairy	–	P		
Alexanders (Black Lovage/ Horse Parsley)	herb	+		M	
Alfalfa Sprouts	nsveg	+		M	
Alligator Pear (Avocado)	nsveg	+		M	
Allspice*	spice	–		M	
Almond Oil*	fats/ oils	n		M	
Almonds*	nuts	+		M	
Alpine Strawberry	fruit	+		O	
Amaranth Seeds	seeds	+		M	
Amchoor (Aamchur/Mango Powder)*	spice	–		M	
America Cress (Land Cress)	nsveg	+		M	

FOOD	FAMILY	+/-/n	PROTEIN	M/O	STARCH
Amia	fruit	+		O	
Anchovies	fish	–	P		
Anelini (must be egg-free)	pasta	–			S
Angelica	herb	+		M	
Angled Loofah or Luffa (Sze Gwa)	nsveg	+		M	
Anise (Aniseed)	herb	+		M	
Anise Seeds (Aniseed)	seeds	+		M	
Apple Cucumber	nsveg	+		M	
Apple Juice	fruit	+		O	
Apple-Berry	fruit	+		O	
Apples	fruit	+		O	
Apricot Fig	fruit	+		O	
Apricot Kernel Oil*	fats/oils	n		M	
Apricots	fruit	+		O	
Arame	nsveg	+		M	
Areca (Betel Nuts)*	nuts	–		M	
Arborio Rice (Risotto Rice)	grains	–			S
Arrowhead Tubers (Chi Gu)	nsveg	+		M	
Arrowroot	grains	+			S
Artichokes	nsveg	+		M	
Arugula (Rocket)	nsveg	+		M	
Asian Breadfruit	fruit	+		O	
Asian Pear (Nashi)	fruit	+		O	
Asparagus	nsveg	–		M	
Asparagus Bean (Yard-Long Bean)	nsveg	+		M	

FOOD	FAMILY	+/-/n	PROTEIN	M/O	STARCH
Asparagus Pea (Winged Bean/Four Angled Bean/Winged Pea)	nsveg	+		M	
Aspic	meat	–	P		
Atta Flour	grains	–			S
Aubergine (Eggplant/Brinjal/ Aigwa)	nsveg	+		M	
Australian Bass	fish	–	P		
Australian Cranesbill	nsveg	+		M	
Avocado (Alligator Pear)	nsveg	+		M	
Avocado Oil*	fats/ oils	n		M	
Awalyuru	fruit	+		O	

B ❧

Babaco (Babacao)	fruit	+		O	
Baby Blue Pumpkin	nsveg	+		M	
Baby Coconut*	nuts	–		M	
Baby Squash (Patty Pan)	nsveg	+		M	
Bacon (organic free-range only)*	meat	–	P		
Bagel	grains	–			S
Baked Beans*	pulses	–			
Balmain Bug	fish	–	P		
Bamboo Fungus	nsveg	+		M	
Bamboo Mustard Cabbage (Chuk Gaai Choi)	nsveg	+		M	

FOOD	FAMILY	+/-/n	PROTEIN	M/O	STARCH
Bamboo Shoots (Chuk Sun)	nsveg	+		M	
Banana	fruit	+		O	
Banana Flour	grains	+			S
Banana Pumpkin	nsveg	+		M	
Bannocks	grains	−			S
Bantam Eggs	eggs/ dairy	−	P		
Bap	grains	−			S
Barbados Sugar (See Added Sweetenings, p.163)					
Barcelona Nuts*	nuts	−		M	
Barley	grains	−			S
Barley Flour	grains	−			S
Barramundi	fish	−	P		
Basil	herb	+		M	
Basmati Rice	grains	−			S
Bass	fish	−	P		
Bastard Cinnamon (Cassia)*	spice	−		M	
Batata (Faan Sue/Sweet Potato)	sveg	+			S
Bay Leaf	herb	+		M	
Bean Sprouts (Dau Nga Choi)	nsveg	+		M	
Beancurd (Tofu/Dau Foo)*	soya	+	P		
Bee Balm (Bergamot/Red Bergamot)	herb	+		M	
Beef (all cuts, but organic/free-range only)	meat	−	P		
Beef Sausages*	meat	−	P		

FOOD	FAMILY	+/-/n	PROTEIN	M/O	STARCH
Beefburgers*	meat	–	P		
Beet Greens	nsveg	+		M	
Beetroot	nsveg	+		M	
Belgian Endive (Chicory)	nsveg	+		M	
Ber (Chinese Apple/Indian Jujube Plum)	fruit	+		O	
Bergamot (Bee Balm/Red Bergamot)	herb	+		M	
Besan (Gram/Chickpea Flour)	grains	–			S
Betel Leaves	herb	+		M	
Betel Nuts (Areca)*	nuts	–		M	
Billabong Tree Fruit	fruit	+		O	
Billy Goat Plum	fruit	+		O	
Bio Yoghurt	eggs/ dairy	+	P		
Biscuits, Savoury	grains	–			S
Biscuits, Sweet*	grains	–			S
Bitter Almonds*	nuts	–		M	
Bitter Gourd (Bitter Melon/ Foo Gwa)	nsveg	+		M	
Black Apple	fruit	+		O	
Black Cherries	fruit	+		O	
Black Bean (Dow See)*	soya	+	P		
Black Kidney Bean (Turtle Bean)*	pulse	–			
Black Lovage (Alexanders/Horse Parsley)	herb	+		M	
Black Olives	fruit	+		O	

FOOD	FAMILY	+/-/n	PROTEIN	M/O	STARCH
Black Onion Seeds (Kalonji/ Nigella)	seeds	+		M	
Black Pepper	condi- ment	–		M	
Black Rye (Pumpernickel)	grains	–			S
Black Sapote (Chocolate Pudding Fruit)	fruit	+		O	
Black Soya Bean (Dow See/Salted Black Bean)*	soya	+	P		
Black-Eyed Bean/Pea (Cowpea/ Catjang)*	pulse	–			
Blackberries	fruit	+		O	
Blackcurrants	fruit	+		O	
Blackfish	fish	–	P		
Blackstrap Molasses (See Added Sweetenings, p.163)					
Blanched Chinese Chives (Gau Wong)	nsveg	+		M	
Blood Orange	fruit	+		O	
Blue Grenadier	fish	–	P		
Blue Max Pumpkin	nsveg	+		M	
Blue Pea (Whole Dried Pea)*	pulse	–			
Blue Quandong Fruit	fruit	+		O	
Blue Threadfin	fish	–	P		
Blueberries	fruit	+		O	
Boab Seeds	seeds	+		M	
Boarfish	fish	–	P		
Bok Choi (Chinese White Cabbage)	nsveg	+		M	

FOOD	FAMILY	+/-/n	PROTEIN	M/O	STARCH
Boletus (Yellow Mushroom)	nsveg	+		M	
Bombay Duck	fish	–	P		
Borage	herb	+		M	
Borecole (Collard/Kale)	nsveg	+		M	
Borlotti Bean (Roman Bean/ Pink Bean)*	pulse	–			
Botargo	fish	–	P		
Bottle Gourd	nsveg	+		M	
Bottle Tree Nuts*	nuts	–		M	
Bowtie Pasta (Farfalle — must be egg-free)	pasta	–			S
Boysenberries	fruit	+		O	
Bracken Root	nsveg	+		M	
Bracken Tip	nsveg	+		M	
Brains	meat	–	P		
Brazil Nuts*	nuts	+		M	
Brazilian Tree Grape (Jaboticaba)	fruit	+		O	
Bread	grains	–			S
Bread Sticks (Grissini)	grains	–			S
Breadcrumbs	grains	–			S
Breadfruit	sveg	+			S
Breadnut Seeds	seeds	+		M	
Breakfast Cereals	grains	–			S
Bream	fish	–	P		
Brill	fish	–	P		
Brinjal (Aubergine/Eggplant/ Aigwa)	nsveg	+		M	

FOOD	FAMILY	+/-/n	PROTEIN	M/O	STARCH
Brioche	grains	–			S
Broad Bean – Dried (Fava Bean)*	pulse	–			
Broad Beans (fresh)	nsveg	+		M	
Broadleaf Batavian Endive (Escarole)	nsveg	+		M	
Broccoflower	nsveg	+		M	
Broccoli	nsveg	+		M	
Brown Bean*	pulse	–			
Brown Bread	grains	–			S
Brown Lentils*	pulse	–			
Brown Mushroom	nsveg	+		M	
Brown Pasta (Wholemeal Pasta – must be egg-free)	pasta	–			S
Brown Rice	grains	–			S
Brussels Sprouts	nsveg	+		M	
Buckwheat	grains	–			S
Buckwheat Flour	grains	–			S
Buffalo	meat	–	P		
Bulgar Wheat (Burghul/Cracked)	grains	–			S
Bullock's Heart Custard Apple	fruit	+		O	
Bunya Bunya Pine Nuts*	nuts	–		M	
Burdekin Plum	fruit	+		O	
Burdock Root	nsveg	+		M	
Burghul Wheat (Bulgar/Cracked)	grains	–			S
Burnet	nsveg	+		M	
Bush Banana	fruit	+		O	
Bush Lemon	fruit	+		O	

FOOD	FAMILY	+/-/n	PROTEIN	M/O	STARCH
Bush Nuts*	nuts	–		M	
Bush Passionfruit	fruit	+		O	
Bush Plum	fruit	+		O	
Bush Potato	sveg	+			S
Bush Raisin	fruit	+		O	
Bush Tomato	fruit	+		O	
Butter*	fats/oils	n		M	
Butter Bean (Lima Bean)*	pulse	–			
Butter Nut*	nuts	–		M	
Butter Pumpkin	nsveg	+		M	
Butterhead Lettuce	nsveg	+		M	
Buttermilk	eggs/dairy	+	P		
Butternut Pumpkin	nsveg	+		M	
Button Mushroom	nsveg	+		M	
Button Onion	nsveg	+		M	

C ∾

FOOD	FAMILY	+/-/n	PROTEIN	M/O	STARCH
Cabbage – Red, Green or White	nsveg	+		M	
Cabbage Tree Palm	nsveg	+		M	
Cactus Fruit (Prickly Pear/ Indian Fig)	fruit	+		O	
Caimito (Star Apple)	fruit	+		O	
Calabrese (Green-Headed Broccoli)	nsveg	+		M	

FOOD	FAMILY	+/–/n	PROTEIN	M/O	STARCH
Calamari (Squid)	fish	–	P		
Calf's Liver	meat	–	P		
Calrose Rice	grains	–			S
Candle Nuts*	nuts	–		M	
Canistel (Egg Fruit/Marmalade Fruit)	fruit	+		O	
Cannellini Bean (Great Northern Bean)*	pulse	–			
Cantaloup Melon	fruit	+		O	
Cape Gooseberry (Physalis)	fruit	+		O	
Capellini (Vermicelli — must be egg-free)	pasta	–			S
Capers*	spice	–		M	
Capsicums (Sweet Peppers/ Tseng Jiu), Green, Red or Yellow	nsveg	+		M	
Carambola (Star Fruit)	fruit	+		O	
Caraway Seeds	seeds	+		M	
Cardamon*	spice	–		M	
Carob Bar* (See Added Sweetenings, p.163)		–			S
Carob Powder* (See Added Sweetenings, p.163)		–			S
Carob Spread* (See Added Sweetenings, p.163)		–			S
Carp	fish	–	P		
Carragheen	nsveg	+		M	
Carrots	nsveg	+		M	
Casaba Melon	fruit	+		O	

FOOD	FAMILY	+/-/n	PROTEIN	M/O	STARCH
Cashew Fruit	fruit	+		O	
Cashew Nuts*	nuts	−		M	
Cassava (Manioc)	sveg	+			S
Cassia (Bastard Cinnamon)*	spice	−		M	
Cassowary Gum Fruit	fruit	+		O	
Catfish	fish	−	P		
Catjang (Black-Eyed Pea/ Bean, Cowpea)*	pulse	−			
Cattle Pumpkin	nsveg	+		M	
Cauliflower (Ye Choi Fa)	nsveg	+		M	
Caviar	fish	−	P		
Cayenne (Chilli)*	spice	+		M	
Cedar Bay Cherry	fruit	+		O	
Celeriac	nsveg	+		M	
Celery (Kunn Choi)	nsveg	+		M	
Celery Cabbage	nsveg	+		M	
Celery Flowering Cabbage	nsveg	+		M	
Celery Salt*	condi-ment	+		M	
Celery Seeds	seeds	+		M	
Cep Mushroom (Cepes)	nsveg	+		M	
Chaat Masala*	spice	−		M	
Chamomile	herb	+		M	
Chanterelle (Egg Mushroom)	nsveg	+		M	
Chapati Flour	grains	−			S
Chapatis	grains	−			S

FOOD	FAMILY	+/–/n	PROTEIN	M/O	STARCH
Chard (Swiss Chard)	nsveg	+		M	
Charentais Melon	fruit	+		O	
Chayote (Choko/Cho Cho/ Vegetable Pear/Hop Jeung Gwa)	nsveg	+		M	
Cheeky Yam	sveg	+			S
Cheese Fruit	fruit	+		O	
Cheeses (all types)	eggs/ dairy	–	P		
Chekur Manis	nsveg	+		M	
Cherimoya Custard Apple	fruit	+		O	
Cherries	fruit	+		O	
Cherries, Glacé*	fruit	–			S
Cherry Plums	fruit	+		O	
Chervil	herb	+		M	
Chestnut Flour	grains	–			S
Chestnut, Sweet (Marron/ Lut Tzee)	nuts	–		M	
Chestnut, Water (Link Gok)	nsveg	+		M	
Chi Gu (Arrowhead Tubers)	nsveg	+		M	
Chicken (free-range only)	meat	–	P		
Chicken's Eggs	eggs/ dairy	–	P		
Chickpea (Garbanzo Bean)*	pulse	–			
Chickpea Flour (Besan/Gram Flour)	grains	–			S
Chicory (Belgian Endive)	nsveg	+		M	
Chilli (Cayenne)*	spice	+		M	

FOOD	FAMILY	+/-/n	PROTEIN	M/O	STARCH
Chilli Peppers*	nsveg	+		M	
Chinese Anise (Star Anise)*	spice	+		M	
Chinese Apple (Ber/Indian Jujube Plum)	fruit	+		O	
Chinese Arrowhead Leaves	nsveg	+		M	
Chinese Black Moss	nsveg	+		M	
Chinese Boxthorn (Gau Gei Choi)	nsveg	+		M	
Chinese Broccoli	nsveg	+		M	
Chinese Cabbage	nsveg	+		M	
Chinese Chives (Garlic Chives/ Gau Choi)	herb	+		M	
Chinese Chives Flowers (Gau Choi Fa)	nsveg	+		M	
Chinese Flat Cabbage (Taai Goo Choi)	nsveg	+		M	
Chinese Flowering Cabbage (Choi Sam)	nsveg	+		M	
Chinese Fuzzy Melon (Tseet Gwa)	nsveg	+		M	
Chinese Gooseberry (Kiwi Fruit)	fruit	+		O	
Chinese Kale (Gaai Laan)	nsveg	+		M	
Chinese Key*	spice	+		M	
Chinese Long Beans (Dau Gok)	nsveg	+		M	
Chinese Mushrooms (Oyster Mushrooms/Pleurotte)	nsveg	+		M	
Chinese Mustard (Mustard Cabbage/Kai Choi)	nsveg	+		M	
Chinese Pea (Mangetout/Snow Peas)	nsveg	+		M	
Chinese Pepper (Szechaun Pepper)*	spice	–		M	

FOOD	FAMILY	+/-/n	PROTEIN	M/O	STARCH
Chinese Radish	nsveg	+		M	
Chinese Red Date	fruit	+		O	
Chinese Spinach (Yin Choi)	nsveg	+		M	
Chinese Water Chestnut	nsveg	+		M	
Chinese White Cabbage (Bok Choi)	nsveg	+		M	
Chinese 5 Spice*	spice	–		M	
Chips (shallow fried in olive oil only)*	sveg	+			S
Chiton	fish	–	P		
Chives	herb	+		M	
Cho Cho (Choko/Chayote/ Hop Jeung Gwa)	nsveg	+		M	
Chocolate (see Foods to Avoid, p.29)					
Chocolate Pudding Fruit (Black Sapote)	fruit	+		O	
Choi Sam (Chinese Flowering Cabbage)	nsveg	+		M	
Chops (all types)	meat	–	P		
Christmas Melon (Santa Claus Melon)	fruit	+		O	
Chuk Gaai Choi (Bamboo Mustard Cabbage)	nsveg	+		M	
Chuk Sun (Bamboo Shoots)	nsveg	+		M	
Chutney* (See Condiments, p.000)					
Ciabatta Bread	grains	–			S
Cider Vinegar*	condi- ment	–		M	

FOOD	FAMILY	+/-/n	PROTEIN	M/O	STARCH
Cilantro (Coriander/Uen Sai)	herb	+		M	
Cinnamon*	spice	–		M	
Citron	fruit	+		O	
Citronen (German Lemon)	fruit	+		O	
Clam	fish	–	P		
Clementines	fruit	+		O	
Cloud Ear Fungus	nsveg	+		M	
Cloudberry	fruit	+		O	
Cloves*	spice	–		M	
Coalfish (Saithe)	fish	–	P		
Cockles	fish	–	P		
Cocky Apple	fruit	+		O	
Cocoa Butter*	fats/oils	n		M	
Coconut*	nuts	–		M	
Coconut, Desiccated*	nuts	–		M	
Coconut Milk*	eggs/dairy	n		M	
Coconut Oil*	fats/oils	n		M	
Cod	fish	–	P		
Cod Liver Oil*	fats/oils	–		M	
Cold Pressed Oils*	fats/oils	n		M	
Cole Leaves	nsveg	+		M	
Coley	fish	–	P		

FOOD	FAMILY	+/-/n	PROTEIN	M/O	STARCH
Collard (Kale/Borecole)	nsveg	+		M	
Colocasi	sveg	+			S
Colony Wattle Seeds	seeds	+		M	
Comfrey	herb	+		M	
Conchigliette (must be egg-free)	pasta	−			S
Condensed Milk	eggs/ dairy	−	P		
Cong Dou (Petah)	nsveg	+		M	
Conkerberry Fruit	fruit	+		O	
Conpoy	fish	−	P		
Continental Lentils (Green Lentils)*	pulse	−			
Cookies*	grains	−			S
Coral Trout	fish	−	P		
Coriander (Cilantro/Uen Sai)	herb	+		M	
Corn (Maize)	sveg	+			S
Corn Oil (Maize Oil)*	fats/ oils	n		M	
Corn on the Cob	sveg	+			S
Cornflour* (See Foods to Avoid, p.29)	grains	−			S
Cornmeal	grains	−			S
Corn Salad (Lamb's Lettuce/ Mache)	nsveg	+		M	
Cos Lettuce (Romaine)	nsveg	+		M	
Cottonseed Oil*	fats/ oils	n		M	
Courgette (Zucchini)	nsveg	+		M	

FOOD	FAMILY	+/-/n	PROTEIN	M/O	STARCH
Couscous	grains	–			S
Cowpea (Black-Eyed Bean/ Pea, Catjang)*	pulse	–			
Cowpea (Fresh Pods)	nsveg	+		M	
Crab	fish	–	P		
Crab Apple	fruit	+		O	
Cracked Wheat (Bulgar/Burghul)	grains	–			S
Crackers (Biscuits, Savoury)	grains	–			S
Cranberries	fruit	+		O	
Crater Aspen Fruit	fruit	+		O	
Crawfish	fish	–	P		
Crayfish	fish	–	P		
Cream (cream is classed as fat not protein)*	fats/ oils	n		M	
Crème Fraîche*	fats/ oils	n		M	
Crenshaw Melon	fruit	+		O	
Cress	nsveg	+		M	
Crispbread	grains	–			S
Crisphead Lettuce	nsveg	+		M	
Croissant	grains	–			S
Crown Prince Pumpkin	nsveg	+		M	
Crumpets	grains	–			S
Crystallized Ginger (See Added Sweetenings, p.163)					
Cucumber (Tseng Gwa)	nsveg	+		M	
Cumin*	spice	–		M	

FOOD	FAMILY	+/-/n	PROTEIN	M/O	STARCH
Cumquat (Kumquat)	fruit	+		O	
Curly Endive	nsveg	+		M	
Curly Kale	nsveg	+		M	
Currant Bush Fruit	fruit	+		O	
Currants	fruit	+		O	
Curry Leaf	herb	+		M	
Curry Powder*	spice	−		M	
Custard Apple	fruit	+		O	
Custard Powder*	grains	−			S
Cuttlefish	fish	−	P		
Cycad	nsveg	+		M	

D ∾

FOOD	FAMILY	+/-/n	PROTEIN	M/O	STARCH
Daai Gaai Choi (Swatow Mustard Cabbage)	nsveg	+		M	
Daai Suen (Leek)	nsveg	+		M	
Dab	fish	−	P		
Dabugay	fruit	+		O	
Daikon (Oriental White Radish/ Loh Baak)	nsveg	+		M	
Dairy Ice Cream	eggs/ dairy	−	P		
Damper	grains	−			S
Damson	fruit	+		O	
Dandelion	herb	+		M	

FOOD	FAMILY	+/-/n	PROTEIN	M/O	STARCH
Dandelion Leaves	nsveg	+		M	
Danish Pastry	grains	−			S
Dark Soy Sauce (Lo Chau)*	condi-ment	−		M	
Dasheen (Eddoes/Taro/Kandalla)	sveg	+			S
Date Plum (Persimmon/Kaki Fruit/ Sharon Fruit)	fruit	+		O	
Dau Foo (Beancurd/Tofu)*	pulse	+	P		
Dau Gok (Chinese Long Beans)	nsveg	+		M	
Dau Miu (Pea Shoots)	nsveg	+		M	
Dau Nga Choi (Bean Sprouts)	nsveg	+		M	
Daun Limau Perut (Lime Leaves)	herb	+		M	
Daun Salam	nsveg	+		M	
Davidson Plum	fruit	+		O	
Desert Acacia Seeds	seeds	+		M	
Dhansak Masala*	spice	−		M	
Dhu-Fish	fish	−	P		
Diamantini (must be egg-free)	pasta	−			S
Dill	herb	+		M	
Dill Seeds	seeds	+		M	
Ditalini (must be egg-free)	pasta	−			S
Dodder Laurel Fruit	fruit	+		O	
Dogfish	fish	−	P		
Dong Gwa (Waxgourd/Winter Melon)	nsveg	+		M	
Dong Gwoo (Shiitaki/Winter Mushrooms)	nsveg	+		M	

FOOD	FAMILY	+/-/n	PROTEIN	M/O	STARCH
Doughnut	grains	−			S
Dover Sole	fish	−	P		
Dow See (Black Soya Bean/ Salted Black Bean)*	soya	−	P		
Dracontomelun (Yun Meen)	fruit	+		O	
Dried Apple	fruit	+		O	
Dried Apricot	fruit	+		O	
Dried Banana	fruit	+		O	
Dried Fig	fruit	+		O	
Dried Fruits (all kinds)	fruit	+		O	
Dried Nectarine	fruit	+		O	
Dried Peach	fruit	+		O	
Dried Pear	fruit	+		O	
Dried Shrimp (Ha Maai)	fish	−	P		
Dripping*	fats/ oils	−		M	
Drummer	fish	−	P		
Drumstick Leaves	nsveg	+		M	
Drumstick Vegetable	nsveg	+		M	
Duck	meat	−	P		
Duck Eggs	eggs/ dairy	−	P		
Dudi	nsveg	+		M	
Dulse	nsveg	+		M	
Dumplings	grains	−			S
Durian	fruit	+		O	
Durum Wheat	grains	−			S

FOOD	FAMILY	+/-/n	PROTEIN	M/O	STARCH

E ∾

FOOD	FAMILY	+/-/n	PROTEIN	M/O	STARCH
Eddoes (Taro/Dasheen/Kandalla)	sveg	+			S
Eel	fish	−	P		
Egg Fruit (Canistel/Marmalade Fruit)	fruit	+		O	
Egg Mushroom (Chanterelle)	nsveg	+		M	
Egg Replacer*	soya	−	P		
Eggplant (Aubergine/Aigwa/Brinjal)	nsveg	+		M	
Eggs (all types)	eggs/dairy	−	P		
Egyptian Brown Bean (Ful Medami)*	pulse	−			
Elderberry	fruit	+		O	
Elderflower	herb	+		M	
Emperor	fish	−	P		
Emu Berry	fruit	+		O	
Emu Eggs	eggs/dairy	−	P		
Endive	nsveg	+		M	
Enoki Mushroom	nsveg	+		M	
Enorkitake Mushroom	nsveg	+		M	
Escarole (Broadleaf Batavian Endive)	nsveg	+		M	
Evaporated Milk	eggs/dairy	−	P		
Ewe's Milk (Sheep's)	eggs/dairy	−	P		

FOOD	FAMILY	+/-/n	PROTEIN	M/O	STARCH
Extra Virgin Olive Oil*	fats/oils	n		M	

F ∾

FOOD	FAMILY	+/-/n	PROTEIN	M/O	STARCH
Faan Sue (Sweet Potato/Batata)	sveg	+			S
Falafel*	pulse	−			
Farfalle (Bowtie Pasta — must be egg-free)	pasta	−			S
Farfallini (must be egg-free)	pasta	−			S
Fava Bean (Broad Bean − Dried)*	pulse	−			
Feijoa (Pineapple Guava)	fruit	+		O	
Fennel Leaves	herb	+		M	
Fennel Seeds (ground)*	spice	+		M	
Fenugreek Seed (sprouts)	nsveg	+		M	
Fenugreek Seeds (ground)*	spice	+		M	
Field Mushroom	nsveg	+		M	
Figs	fruit	+		O	
Filberts (Hazelnuts)*	nuts	−		M	
Fillet Steak (beef)	meat	−	P		
Finger Lime	fruit	+		O	
Flageolet Bean*	pulse	−			
Flame Tree Seeds	seeds	+		M	
Flat Swamp Potato	sveg	+			S
Flathead	fish	−	P		
Flax Lily	sveg	+			S

FOOD	FAMILY	+/-/n	PROTEIN	M/O	STARCH
Flaxseed Oil (Linseed Oil)*	fats/oils	n		M	
Flounder	fish	–	P		
Flour (all types)	grains	–			S
Focaccia (must be egg-free)	pasta	–			S
Foo Gwa (Bitter Gourd/Melon)	nsveg	+		M	
Four Angled Bean (Pea/Winged Bean/Asparagus Pea)	nsveg	+		M	
French Beans	nsveg	+		M	
Fresh Pods (Cowpea)	nsveg	+		M	
Freshwater Mussels	fish	–	P		
Fringe Rush Seeds	seeds	+		M	
Frog's Legs	meat	–	P		
Fromage Frais	eggs/dairy	+	P		
Fruit Juices (all types)	fruit	+		O	
Fruit Sugar (fructose) (See Added Sweetenings, p.163)					
Ful Medami (Egyptian Brown Bean)*	pulse	–			
Fungi	nsveg	+		M	
Fun Got (Kudzu Root)	sveg	+			S
Fun See (Mung Bean Vermicelli)*	pulse	–			
Fusilli (must be egg-free)	pasta	–			S

FOOD	FAMILY	+/–/n	PROTEIN	M/O	STARCH

G ∾

FOOD	FAMILY	+/–/n	PROTEIN	M/O	STARCH
Gaai Laan (Chinese Kale, Kailan)	nsveg	+		M	
Gaai Laan Tau (Kohlrabi)	nsveg	+		M	
Gaau Sun (Wild Rice Shoots)	herb	+		M	
Galangal*	spice	–		M	
Galia Melon	fruit	+		O	
Gammon	meat	–	P		
Garam Masala*	spice	–		M	
Garbanzo Bean (Chickpea)*	pulse	–			
Garfish	fish	–	P		
Gari (Cassava – Dried)	grains	=			S
Garland Chrysanthemum (Tong Ho)	nsveg	+		M	
Garlic (Suan Tau)	herb	+		M	
Garlic Salt*	condi-ment	+		M	
Gau Choi (Chinese Chives/ Garlic Chives)	herb	+		M	
Gau Choi Fa (Chinese Chives Flowers)	nsveg	+		M	
Gau Gei Choi (Chinese Boxthorn)	nsveg	+		M	
Gau Wong (Blanched Chinese Chives)	nsveg	+		M	
Geebung	fruit	+		O	
Gelatin	meat	–	P		
Gemfish	fish	–	P		
German Lemon (Citronen)	fruit	+		O	

FOOD	FAMILY	+/-/n	PROTEIN M/O	STARCH
Gherkin Cucumber (fresh only, not pickled)	nsveg	+	M	
Ginger, Crystallized (See Added Sweetenings, p.163)				
Ginger, fresh stem (Tsee Geung)*	spice	−	M	
Ginger, ground (Geung)*	spice	−	M	
Ginkgo Nuts*	nuts	−	M	
Globe Artichoke	nsveg	+	M	
Glucose Powder (See Foods to Avoid, p.29)				
Glutinous Rice	grains	−		S
Gnocchetti (must be egg-free)	pasta	−		S
Gnocchi (must be egg-free)	pasta	−		S
Goanna	meat	−	P	
Goat's Milk	eggs/ dairy	−	P	
Goat's Yoghurt	eggs/ dairy	+	P	
Golden Nugget Pumpkin	nsveg	+	M	
Golden Syrup (See Foods to Avoid, p.29)				
Gomasio (Sesame Salt)*	condi- ment	−	M	
Good King Henry (Poor Man's Asparagus)	nsveg	+	M	
Goose	meat	−	P	
Goose Eggs	eggs/ dairy	−	P	
Gooseberries	fruit	+	O	
Gourd	nsveg	+	M	

FOOD	FAMILY	+/-/n	PROTEIN	M/O	STARCH
Gram Flour (Besan/Chickpea Flour)	grains	–			S
Gramigna (must be egg-free)	pasta	–			S
Granadillas (Passion Fruit)	fruit	+		O	
Granary Bread	grains	–			S
Grape Juice (all types)	fruit	+		O	
Grapefruit	fruit	+		O	
Grapefruit Juice	fruit	+		O	
Grapes (all types)	fruit	+		O	
Grapeseed Oil*	fats/oils	n		M	
Grass Potato	sveg	+			S
Great Northern Bean (Cannellini Bean)*	pulse	–			
Greek Yoghurt	eggs/dairy	+	P		
Green Ginger Fruit	fruit	+		O	
Green Gram (Mung Bean/Moong Dal)*	pulse	–			
Green-Headed Broccoli (Calabrese)	nsveg	+		M	
Green-Headed Cauliflower (Romanesco)	nsveg	+		M	
Green Lentils (Continental Lentils)*	pulse	–			
Green Olives	fruit	+		O	
Green Onions (Scallions/Spring Onions)	nsveg	+		M	
Green Pea Flour	grains	–			S
Green Plum	fruit	+		O	

FOOD	FAMILY	+/-/n	PROTEIN	M/O	STARCH
Greengages	fruit	+		O	
Grissini (Bread Sticks)	grains	–			S
Grits	grains	–			S
Groper	fish	–	P		
Ground Almonds*	nuts	–		M	
Ground Rice	grains	–			S
Groundnut (Peanut; organic only)*	pulse	–			
Grouse	meat	–	P		
Guava	fruit	+		O	
Guinea Fowl	meat	–	P		
Guinea Fowl Eggs	eggs/ dairy	–	P		
Gumbo (Okra/Ladies' Fingers)	nsveg	+		M	
Gundabluey Seeds	seeds	+		M	
Gurnard	fish	–	P		

H ∾

FOOD	FAMILY	+/-/n	PROTEIN	M/O	STARCH
Ha Maai (Dried Shrimp)	fish	–	P		
Haam Daan (Salted Duck Eggs)	eggs/ dairy	–	P		
Haddock	fish	–	P		
Haggis (See Foods to Avoid, p.29)					
Hairtail	fish	–	P		
Hake	fish	–	P		
Halibut	fish	–	P		

FOOD	FAMILY	+/–/n	PROTEIN	M/O	STARCH
Halibut Liver Oil*	fats/oils	–		M	
Ham (organic, free-range only)*	meat	–	P		
Hare	meat	–	P		
Haricot Bean (Navy Bean)*	pulse	–			
Hatcho Miso*	soya	–	P		
Hazelnut Oil*	fats/oils	n		M	
Hazelnuts (Filberts)*	nuts	–		M	
Head Cabbage (Yeh Choi)	nsveg	+		M	
Heart	meat	–	P		
Hen's Eggs	eggs dairy	– –	P		
Herring	fish	–	P		
Hijiki	nsveg	+		M	
Hoke	fish	–	P		
Hominy (Maize Grits)	grains	–			S
Honey (cold pressed only) (See Added Sweetenings, p.163)					
Honeydew Melon	fruit	+		O	
Hops	herb	+		M	
Hop Jeung Gwa (Chayote/Choko/Cho Cho/Vegetable Pear)	nsveg	+		M	
Horned Melon (Kiwano)	fruit	+		O	
Horse Parsley (Alexanders/Black Lovage)	herb	+		M	
Horseradish*	spice	–		M	
Hot Cross Bun	grains	–			S

FOOD	FAMILY	+/-/n	PROTEIN	M/O	STARCH
Ho Yau (Oyster Sauce)*	condiment	–		M	
Hubbard Pumpkin (Hubbard Squash)	nsveg	+		M	
Huckleberries	fruit	+		O	
Hummus (made from chickpeas)*	pulse	–			
Hunza Apricots	fruit	+		O	
Hussar	fish	–	P		
Hyacinth Bean (Lablab)*	pulse	–			
Hyssop	herb	+		M	

I ∾

FOOD	FAMILY	+/-/n	PROTEIN	M/O	STARCH
Ice Cream, Dairy	eggs/dairy	–	P		
Iceberg Lettuce	nsveg	+		M	
Ikan Bilis	fish	–	P		
Indian Almonds*	nuts	–		M	
Indian Borage	herb	+		M	
Indian Date (Tamarind)	fruit	+		O	
Indian Fig (Cactus Fruit/ Prickly Pear)	fruit	+		O	
Indian Jujube Plum (Ber/ Chinese Apple)	fruit	+		O	
Italian Rice	grains	–			S

FOOD	FAMILY	+/-/n	PROTEIN	M/O	STARCH

J ❧

FOOD	FAMILY	+/-/n	PROTEIN	M/O	STARCH
Jaboticaba (Brazilian Tree Grape)	fruit	+		O	
Jackfruit	fruit	+		O	
Jam (See Foods to Avoid, p.29)					
Jamaican Red Tilapia	fish	–	P		
Jambu Fruit	fruit	+		O	
Japanese Medlar (Loquat)	fruit	+		O	
Jarrahdale Pumpkin	nsveg	+		M	
Jasmine Rice (Thai Fragrant Rice)	grains	–			S
Java Plum (Tamarillo)	fruit	+		O	
Jelly (Jello) (See Foods to Avoid, p.29)					
Jellyfish (edible)	fish	–	P		
Jerusalem Artichoke	nsveg	+		M	
Jewfish (Mulloway)	fish	–	P		
Jew's Ear Mushrooms (Wan Yee)	nsveg	+		M	
Jew's Mallow (Melokhia)	sveg	+			S
Jicama (Yam Bean/Sha Ge)	sveg	+			S
Jiu La Choi (Sow Cabbage)	nsveg	+		M	
John Dory	fish	–	P		
Johnstone River Almonds*	nuts	–		M	
Juniper	herb	+		M	
Juniper Berries	fruit	+		O	
Junn Jiu Choi (White Wormwood)	nsveg	+		M	
Jurdal	fruit	+		O	

FOOD	FAMILY	+/-/n	PROTEIN	M/O	STARCH
K ∾					
Kai Choi (Mustard Cabbage/ Chinese Mustard)	nsveg	+		M	
Kaki Fruit (Persimmon/ Date Plum/Sharon Fruit)	fruit	+		O	
Kalamansi	fruit	+		O	
Kale (Collard/Borecole)	nsveg	+		M	
Kalonji (Nigella/Black Onion Seeds)	seeds	+		M	
Kalumburu Yam	sveg	+			S
Kamut	grains	−			S
Kandalla (Eddoes/Taro/Dasheen)	sveg	+			S
Kang Kong (Water Spinach/ Ong Choi)	nsveg	+		M	
Kasha (Roasted Buckwheat)	grains	−			S
Kashmiri Masala*	spice	−		M	
Kelp	nsveg	+		M	
Ketchup (Catsup) (See Foods to Avoid, p.29)					
Ketumbar Jawa	herb	−		M	
Kidney	meat	−	P		
Kidney Bean*	pulse	−			
King Orchid	sveg	+			S
Kingfish	fish	−	P		
Kipper	fish	−	P		
Kiwano Melon (African Horned Melon)	fruit	+		O	
Kiwi Fruit (Chinese Gooseberry)	fruit	+		O	

FOOD	FAMILY	+/-/n	PROTEIN	M/O	STARCH
Kohlrabi (Gaai Laan Tau)	nsveg	+		M	
Kombu	nsveg	+		M	
Kudzu Root (Fun Got)	sveg	+			S
Kuichai Onion	nsveg	+		M	
Kumara Sweet Potato	sveg	+			S
Kumquat (Cumquat)	fruit	+		O	
Kunn Choi (Celery)	nsveg	+		M	
Kurau	fish	−	P		
Kurrajong*	nuts	−		M	
Kuzu Powder	grains	−			S

L ∾

Lablab (Hyacinth Bean)*	pulse	−			
Ladies' Fingers (Okra/Gumbo)	nsveg	+		M	
Laksa	herb	−		M	
Lamb (all cuts)	meat	−	P		
Lamb's Kidney	meat	−	P		
Lamb's Lettuce (Mache/Corn Salad)	nsveg	+		M	
Lamb's Liver	meat	−	P		
Land Cress (America Cress)	nsveg	+		M	
Langoustine	fish	−	P		
Lard*	fats/ oils	−		M	
Lasagne (without protein filling)	pasta	−			S

FOOD	FAMILY	+/-/n	PROTEIN	M/O	STARCH
Lavan Melon	fruit	+		O	
Lavash	grains	–			S
Laver (Nori/Sloke/Slake)	nsveg	+		M	
Lawyer Vine Fruit	fruit	+		O	
Leaf Lettuce	nsveg	+		M	
Leatherjacket	fish	–	P		
Leek (Daai Suen)	nsveg	+		M	
Leen Ngau (Lotus Tubers)	nsveg	+		M	
Lemon Balm	herb	+		M	
Lemon Grass	herb	+		M	
Lemon Juice	fruit	+		O	
Lemon Sole	fish	–	P		
Lemon Thyme	herb	+		M	
Lemon Verbena	herb	+		M	
Lemons	fruit	+		O	
Lentil Flour	grains	–			S
Lentils (all types)*	pulse	–			
Lettuce (all types)	nsveg	+		M	
Light Soy Sauce (See Yau)*	condiment			M	
Lights	meat	–	P		
Lillypilly Fruits	fruit	+		O	
Lima Bean (Butter Bean)*	pulse	–			
Lime Flowers	herb	+		M	
Lime Juice	fruit	+		O	
Lime Leaves (Daun Limau Perut)	herb	+		M	

FOOD	FAMILY	+/-/n	PROTEIN	M/O	STARCH
Limes	fruit	+		O	
Limetta (Sweet Lime)	fruit	+		O	
Ling	fish	–	P		
Linguine (must be egg-free)	pasta	–			S
Link Gok (Water Chestnut)	nsveg	+		M	
Linseed Oil (Flaxseed Oil)*	fats/oils	n		M	
Linseeds	seeds	+		M	
Liquorice*	herb	–		M	
Liver	meat	–	P		
Lizard	meat	–	P		
Lobster	fish	–	P		
Lo Chau (Dark Soy Sauce)*	condiment	–		M	
Loganberries	fruit	+		O	
Loh Baak (Oriental White Radish/ Daikon)	nsveg	+		M	
Lollo Rosso	nsveg	+		M	
Long Grain Rice	grains	–			S
Long Yam	sveg	+			S
Longans	fruit	+		O	
Loquat (Japanese Medlar)	fruit	+		O	
Lotus Root Starch	grains	–			S
Lotus Seeds	seeds	+		M	
Lotus Tubers (Leen Ngau)	nsveg	+		M	
Lovage (Sea Parsley)	herb	+		M	

FOOD	FAMILY	+/-/n	PROTEIN	M/O	STARCH
Lupin Bean*	pulse	–			
Lut Tzee (Marron/Sweet Chestnuts)*	nuts	–		M	
Lychees	fruit	+		O	

M ∾

FOOD	FAMILY	+/-/n	PROTEIN	M/O	STARCH
Macadamia Nuts (Queensland Nuts)*	nuts	–		M	
Macadamia Oil*	fats/oils	n		M	
Macapuno*	nuts	–		M	
Macaroni (must be egg-free)	pasta	–			S
Mace*	spice	–		M	
Mache (Lamb's Lettuce/Corn Salad)	nsveg	+		M	
Mackerel	fish	–	P		
Mahlab*	spice	–		M	
Maize (Corn)	sveg	+			S
Maize Flour	grains	–			S
Maize Grits (Hominy)	grains	–			S
Maize Oil (Corn Oil)*	fats/oils	n		M	
Malaga Bean Fruit	fruit	+		O	
Malanga	sveg	+			S
Malt Flour	grains	–			S
Malt Vinegar (See Foods to Avoid, p.29)					
Mammie Apple	fruit	+		O	

FOOD	FAMILY	+/-/n	PROTEIN	M/O	STARCH
Mandarins	fruit	+		O	
Mangetout (Snow Peas/ Chinese Pea)	nsveg	+		M	
Mango Juice	fruit	+		O	
Mangos	fruit	+		O	
Mangosteen	fruit	+		O	
Manioc (Cassava)	sveg	+			S
Maple Syrup (real, natural only) (See Added Sweetenings, p.163)					
Margarine*	fats/ oils	n		M	
Marjoram	herb	+		M	
Marmalade (See Foods to Avoid, p.29)					
Marmalade Fruit (Egg Fruit/ Canistel)	fruit	+		O	
Marron (Sweet Chestnuts/ Lut Tzee)*	nuts	−		M	
Marrow	nsveg	+		M	
Marrowfat Peas*	pulse	−			
Matoki	sveg	+			S
Matsutake Mushrooms	nsveg	+		M	
Matzo	grains	−			S
Matzo Meal	grains	−			S
Mayonnaise (See Condiments, p.161)					
Meat Pasties (See Foods to Avoid, p.29)					
Medlars	fruit	+		O	
Megrim	fish	−	P		
Mekabu	nsveg	+		M	

FOOD	FAMILY	+/-/n	PROTEIN	M/O	STARCH
Melokhia (Jew's Mallow)	sveg	+			S
Melon Seeds	seeds	+		M	
Melons (all types)	fruit	+		O	
Midjin	fruit	+		O	
Milk – Pasturised*	eggs/ dairy	–	P		
Milk – Unpasturised*	eggs/ dairy	+	P		
Millet	grains	+			S
Millet Flour	grains	+			S
Mint	herb	+		M	
Miso*	soya	–	P		
Mixed Peel	fruit	+		O	
Mixed Spice*	spice	–		M	
Mongo	fruit	+		O	
Monkfish	fish	–	P		
Moong Dal (Mung Bean/ Green Gram)*	pulse	–			
Morel (Sponge Mushroom)	nsveg	+		M	
Moreton Bay Bug	fish	–	P		
Mud Crab	fish	–	P		
Muesli	grains	–			S
Muffin	grains	–			S
Mugi Miso*	soya	–	P		
Mulberries	fruit	+		O	
Mulga Seeds	seeds	+		M	

FOOD	FAMILY	+/-/n	PROTEIN	M/O	STARCH
Mullet, Red and Grey	fish	–	P		
Mulloway (Jewfish)	fish	–	P		
Mung Bean (Green Gram/ Moong Dal)*	pulse	–			
Mungbean Vermicelli (Fun See)*	pulse	–			
Mushrooms	nsveg	+		M	
Mushy Peas*	pulse	–			
Mussels	fish	–	P		
Mussels, Freshwater	fish	–	P		
Mustard & Cress	nsveg	+		M	
Mustard (ground)*	spice	–		M	
Mustard Cabbage (Chinese Mustard/Kai Choi)	nsveg	+		M	
Mustard Greens	nsveg	+		M	
Mustard Oil*	fats/ oils	n		M	
Mustard Seeds	seeds	+		M	
Mutton	meat	–	P		
Myrtle	herb	+		M	

N ∾

Naan	grains	–			S
Nameko	nsveg	+		M	
Napa (Peking Cabbage)	nsveg	+		M	
Narrow-Leaf Bumble	fruit	+		O	

FOOD	FAMILY	+/-/n	PROTEIN	M/O	STARCH
Nashi (Asian Pear)	fruit	+		O	
Nasturtium	nsveg	+		M	
Native Banana	fruit	+		O	
Native Capers (Wild Orange)	fruit	+		O	
Native Cucumber Fruit	fruit	+		O	
Native Grape	fruit	+		O	
Native Guava	fruit	+		O	
Native Melon	fruit	+		O	
Native Millet	seeds	+		M	
Native Onion	nsveg	+		M	
Navel Orange (Winter/ Seville Orange)	fruit	+		O	
Navy Bean (Haricot Bean)*	pulse	−			
Nectarines	fruit	+		O	
Nettle	herb	+		M	
Nettles	nsveg	+		M	
New Zealand Spinach	nsveg	+		M	
Nigella (Black Onion Seeds/ Kalonji)	seeds	+		M	
Nipan	fruit	+		O	
Nonda Plum	fruit	+		O	
Noodles (must be egg-free)	pasta	−			S
Nori (Laver/Sloke/Slake)	nsveg	+		M	
Northern Kurrajong Seeds	seeds	+		M	
Nutbush Nuts*	nuts	−		M	
Nutmeg*	spice	−		M	

FOOD	FAMILY	+/-/n	PROTEIN	M/O	STARCH
Nuts (all acid-forming except Almonds and Brazils)	nuts	–		M	
Nypa Palm Fruit	fruit	+		O	

O ∾

Oakleaf Lettuce	nsveg	+		M	
Oarweed	nsveg	+		M	
Oat Biscuits	grains	–			S
Oat Cakes	grains	–			S
Oat Flour	grains	–			S
Oatgerm	grains	–			S
Oatmeal	grains	–			S
Oats (rolled/porridge)	grains	–			S
Ocean Perch (Orange Roughy)	fish	–	P		
Octopus	fish	–	P		
Offal	meat	–	P		
Ogen Melon	fruit	+		O	
Okara (Soya Fibre)*	soya	–	P		
Okra (Ladies' Fingers/Gumbo)	nsveg	+		M	
Olives (all types)	fruit	+		O	
Ong Choi (Kang Kong/Water Spinach)	nsveg	+		M	
Onion	nsveg	+		M	
Orange Juice	fruit	+		O	
Orange Roughy (Ocean Perch)	fish	–	P		

FOOD	FAMILY	+/-/n	PROTEIN	M/O	STARCH
Oranges	fruit	+		O	
Orecchiette (must be egg-free)	pasta	−			S
Oregano	herb	+		M	
Oriental Green Radish (Tseng Loh Baak)	nsveg	+		M	
Oriental White Radish (Daikon/Loh Baak)	nsveg	+		M	
Ortaniques	fruit	+		O	
Ostrich Eggs	eggs/dairy	−	P		
Ox Tail	meat	−	P		
Oyster Mushroom (Chinese Mushroom/Pleurotte)	nsveg	+		M	
Oyster Plant (Salsify)	nsveg	+		M	
Oyster Sauce (Ho Yau)*	condiment	−		M	
Oysters	fish	−	P		

P ❧

Pak Choi Cabbage	nsveg	+		M	
Palm Heart	nsveg	+		M	
Palm Nuts*	nuts	−		M	
Palm Oil*	fats/oils	n		M	
Pandanus	fruit	+		O	
Pandanus Nuts*	nuts	−		M	

FOOD	FAMILY	+/-/n	PROTEIN	M/O	STARCH
Panettone	grains	−			S
Papaya (Paw-Paw)	fruit	+		O	
Pappadum	grains	−			S
Paprika*	spice	−		M	
Parakeelya Leaves	nsveg	+		M	
Parakeelya Seeds	seeds	+		M	
Parasole Mushroom	nsveg	+		M	
Paratha	grains	−			S
Parrot Fish	fish	−	P		
Parsley	herb	+		M	
Parsnips	nsveg	+		M	
Partridge	meat	−	P		
Passion Fruit (Granadillas)	fruit	+		O	
Passion Fruit Juice	fruit	+		O	
Pasta (must be egg-free)	pasta	−			S
Pasties, Meat (See Foods to Avoid, p.29)					
Pastry (all types)	grains	−			S
Pâté (fish or meat)	fish/ meat	−	P		
Patra Leaves	nsveg	+		M	
Patty Pan (Baby Squash)	nsveg	+		M	
Paw-Paw (Papaya)	fruit	+		O	
Pea Shoots (Dau Miu)	nsveg	+		M	
Peaches	fruit	+		O	
Peanut (Groundnut, organic only)*	pulse	−			
Peanut Butter (organic only)*	pulse	−			

FOOD	FAMILY	+/-/n	PROTEIN	M/O	STARCH
Pearl Barley	grains	−			S
Pears	fruit	+		O	
Peas (fresh)	nsveg	+		M	
Pease Pudding*	pulse	−			
Pecan Nuts*	nuts	−		M	
Pecan Oil*	fats/ oils	n		M	
Pei Daan (Preserved Duck Eggs)	eggs/ dairy	−	P		
Peking Cabbage (Napa)	nsveg	+		M	
Pencil Yam	sveg	+			S
Penne (must be egg-free)	pasta	−			S
Penny Royal	herb	+		M	
Pepino	fruit	+		O	
Pepitas (Pumpkin Seeds)	seeds	+		M	
Peppercorns*	condi- ment	−		M	
Peppermint	herb	+		M	
Peppers, Sweet Bell, Green, Red or Yellow (Capsicums)	nsveg	+		M	
Perch	fish	−	P		
Persian Melon	fruit	+		O	
Persimmon (Date Plum/ Kaki Fruit/Sharon Fruit)	fruit	+		O	
Pesto (pesto sauce)*	nuts	−		M	
Petah (Cong Dou)	nsveg	+		M	
Petit Pois	nsveg	+		M	

FOOD	FAMILY	+/-/n	PROTEIN	M/O	STARCH
Pheasant	meat	−	P		
Pheasant Eggs	eggs/dairy	−	P		
Physalis (Cape Gooseberry)	fruit	+		O	
Pigeon	meat	−	P		
Pigeon Pea*	pulse	−			
Pigface Fruit	fruit	+		O	
Pigface Leaves	nsveg	+		M	
Pig's Liver (See Foods to Avoid, p.29)					
Pig's Trotters (organic, free-range only)	meat	−	P		
Pike	fish	−	P		
Pilchard	fish	−	P		
Pine Nuts (Pine Kernels)*	nuts	−		M	
Pineapple	fruit	+		O	
Pineapple Guava (Feijoa)	fruit	+		O	
Pineapple Juice	fruit	+		O	
Pink Bean (Borlotti Bean/ Roman Bean)*	pulse	−			
Pinto Bean*	pulse	−			
Pistachios*	nuts	−		M	
Pitagna (Surinam Cherry)	fruit	+		O	
Pitta	grains	−			S
Pizza (base only)	grains	−			S
Plaice	fish	−	P		
Plantain	fruit	+		O	

FOOD	FAMILY	+/-/n	PROTEIN	M/O	STARCH
Pleurotte (Oyster Mushroom/ Chinese Mushroom)	nsveg	+		M	
Pluster Fig	fruit	+		O	
Pointed Head Cabbage	nsveg	+		M	
Polenta	grains	−			S
Polyunsaturated Spreads (Non-hydrogenated only)*	fats/ oils	n		M	
Pomegranate	fruit	+		O	
Pomelo (Shaddock)	fruit	+		O	
Popcorn	grains	−			S
Poppy Seeds	seeds	+		M	
Porcini (Wild Mushroom)	nsveg	+		M	
Porgy	fish	−	P		
Pork (all cuts; organic, free-range only)*	meat	−	P		
Pork Pies (See Foods to Avoid, p.29)					
Pork Sausages (organic, free-range, starch-free)	meat	−	P		
Porridge	grains	−			S
Pot Barley (Scotch Barley)	grains	−			S
Potato	sveg	+			S
Potato Flour	grains	+			S
Potato Orchid	sveg	+			S
Powdered Milk	eggs/ dairy	−	P		
Prawns	fish	−	P		
Preserved Duck Eggs (Pei Daan)	eggs/ dairy	−	P		

FOOD	FAMILY	+/-/n	PROTEIN	M/O	STARCH
Pretzels	grains	−			S
Prickly Pear (Cactus Fruit/ Indian Fig)	fruit	+		O	
Prune	fruit	+		O	
Prune Juice	fruit	+		O	
Puff Ball	nsveg	+		M	
Pullet Eggs	eggs/ dairy	−	P		
Pumpernickel (Black Rye)	grains	−			S
Pumpkin	nsveg	+		M	
Pumpkin Seed Oil*	fats/ oils	n		M	
Pumpkin Seeds (Pepitas)	seeds	+		M	
Puri	grains	−			S
Purple Sprouting Broccoli	nsveg	+		M	
Purslane	herb	+		M	

Q

Quail	meat	−	P		
Quail Eggs	eggs/ dairy	−	P		
Quandong*	nuts	−		M	
Queensland Blue Pumpkin	nsveg	+		M	
Queensland Nuts (Macadamia Nuts)*	nuts	−		M	
Quince	fruit	+		O	
Quinoa	grains	−			S

FOOD	FAMILY	+/-/n	PROTEIN	M/O	STARCH

R ～

FOOD	FAMILY	+/-/n	PROTEIN	M/O	STARCH
Raajma (Red Kidney Bean)*	pulse	−			
Rabbit	meat	−	P		
Radicchio Chicory	nsveg	+		M	
Radishes, White and Red	nsveg	+		M	
Ragah	fruit	+		O	
Rainbow Trout	fish	−	P		
Raisins	fruit	+		O	
Rambutan	fruit	+		O	
Rapeseed Oil*	fats/ oils	n		M	
Raspberries	fruit	+		O	
Ray	fish	−	P		
Red Bopple Nuts*	nuts	−		M	
Red Cabbage	nsveg	+		M	
Red Flowered Kurrajong Seeds	seeds	+		M	
Red Kidney Bean (Raajma)*	pulse	−			
Red Lentils (Split Lentils)*	pulse	−			
Red Onions	nsveg	+		M	
Red Palm Oil*	fats/ oils	n		M	
Red Rice	grains	−			S
Red Sweet Potato	sveg	+			S
Redcurrants	fruit	+		O	
Redfish	fish	−	P		
Reishi Mushroom	nsveg	+		M	

FOOD	FAMILY	+/–/n	PROTEIN	M/O	STARCH
Rhubarb (See Foods to Avoid, p.29)					
Rice (all types)	grains	–			S
Rice Bran	grains	–			S
Rice, Brown	grains	–			S
Rice Cakes	grains	–			S
Rice Flour	grains	–			S
Rice, Long Grain	grains	–			S
Rice Noodles	grains	–			S
Rice, Short Grain	grains	–			S
Rice, White	grains	–			S
Ricebran Oil*	fats/oils	n		M	
Risotto Rice (Arborio Rice)	grains	–			S
Rissoni (must be egg-free)	pasta	–			S
Roasted Buckwheat (Kasha)	grains	–			S
Rock Melon	fruit	+		O	
Rock Osyters	fish	–	P		
Rock Salt*	condiment	+		M	
Rocket (Arugula)	nsveg	+		M	
Roe (all types)	fish	–	P		
Rolls	grains	–			S
Romaine Lettuce (Cos)	nsveg	+		M	
Roman Bean (Borlotti Bean)*	pulse	–			
Romanesco (Green-Headed Cauliflower)	nsveg	+		M	

FOOD	FAMILY	+/-/n	PROTEIN	M/O	STARCH
Rose Coco Bean*	pulse	−			
Rose Hips	fruit	+		O	
Rosemary	herb	+		M	
Ruby Saltbush Fruit	fruit	+		O	
Rump Steak (beef)	meat	−	P		
Runner Beans	nsveg	+		M	
Rutabaga (Swede)	nsveg	+		M	
Rye	grains	−			S
Rye Bread	grains	−			S
Rye Crispbread	grains	−			S
Rye Flour	grains	−			S

S 🙌

FOOD	FAMILY	+/-/n	PROTEIN	M/O	STARCH
Saan Choi (Slippery Vegetable Leaves)	nsveg	+		M	
Safflower Oil*	fats/oils	n		M	
Saffron*	spice	−		M	
Sage	herb	+		M	
Sago	grains	−			S
Saithe (Coalfish)	fish	−	P		
Sai Yeung Choi (Water Cress)	nsveg	+		M	
Salad Burnet	herb	+		M	
Salad Cream (See Condiments, p.161)					
Salami	meat	−	P		

FOOD	FAMILY	+/-/n	PROTEIN	M/O	STARCH
Salep Powder	grains	−			S
Salmon	fish	−	P		
Salmon Trout	fish	−	P		
Salsify (Oyster Plant)	nsveg	+		M	
Salt*	condi-ment	+		M	
Salt Substitutes*	condi-ment	+		M	
Salted Black Bean (Black Soya Bean/Dow See)*	soya	+	P		
Salted Duck Eggs (Haam Daan)	eggs/dairy	−	P		
Samphire	nsveg	+		M	
Sambar Masala*	spice	−		M	
Sand Palm	nsveg	+		M	
Sandalwood Nuts*	nuts	−		M	
Sandpaper Fig	fruit	+		O	
Sansho Powder*	spice	−		M	
Santa Claus Melon (Christmas Melon)	fruit	+		O	
Sapodilla	fruit	+		O	
Sardine	fish	−	P		
Satsumas	fruit	+		O	
Sauerkraut	nsveg	+		M	
Sausages (all types; starch-free)*	meat	−	P		
Saveloy (smoked sausage) (See Foods to Avoid, p.29)					
Savory	herb	+		M	

FOOD	FAMILY	+/-/n	PROTEIN	M/O	STARCH
Savoy Cabbage	nsveg	+		M	
Saw Sedge Seeds	seeds	+		M	
Scallions (Spring/Green Onions)	nsveg	+		M	
Scallop	fish	−	P		
Scampi (without breadcrumbs only)	fish	−	P		
Scotch Barley (Pot Barley)	grains	−			S
Screw Pine	nsveg	+		M	
Sea Bream	fish	−	P		
Sea Cucumber	fish	−	P		
Sea Kale	nsveg	+		M	
Sea Lettuce	nsveg	+		M	
Sea Parsley (Lovage)	nsveg	+		M	
Sea Salt*	condi-ment	+		M	
Sea Trout	fish	−	P		
Sea Urchin	fish	−	P		
Seagull Eggs	eggs/dairy	−	P		
Seaweed (all types)	nsveg	+		M	
See Yau (Light Soy Sauce)*	condi-ment	−		M	
Seitan (Zeitan)	grains	−			S
Selar	fish	−	P		
Semolina	grains	−			S
Sesame Oil*	fats/oils	n		M	
Sesame Salt (Gomasio)*	condi-ment	+		M	

FOOD	FAMILY	+/–/n	PROTEIN	M/O	STARCH
Sesame Seed Paste (Tahini)	seeds	+		M	
Sesame Seeds	seeds	+		M	
Seville Orange (Winter/Navel Orange)	fruit	+		O	
Shaddock (Pomelo)	fruit	+		O	
Sha Ge (Yam Bean/Jicama)	sveg	+			S
Shallots (Ts'ung Tau)	nsveg	+		M	
Shark	fish	–	P		
Sharon Fruit (Persimmon/Date Plum/Kaki Fruit)	fruit	+		O	
Sheep's Milk (Ewe's)	eggs/dairy	–	P		
Sheep's Yoghurt	eggs/dairy	+	P		
Shiitaki (Winter Mushrooms/Dong Gwoo)	nsveg	+		M	
Shiso	herb	+		M	
Shortening*	fats/oils	–		M	
Short Grain Rice	grains	–			S
Shrimps	fish	–	P		
Shu Yu (Yam)	sveg	+			S
Silama Spinach	nsveg	+		M	
Silverbeet	nsveg	+		M	
Sirloin Steak (beef)	meat	–	P		
Skate	fish	–	P		
Slake (Nori/Sloke/Laver)	nsveg	+		M	

FOOD	FAMILY	+/-/n	PROTEIN	M/O	STARCH
Slippery Vegetable Leaves (Saan Choi)	nsveg	+		M	
Sloke (Slake/Nori/Laver)	nsveg	+		M	
Smetana	eggs/ dairy	–	P		
Smoked Fish (any)*	fish	–	P		
Smoked Meats (any) (See Foods to Avoid, p.29)					
Smoked Salmon*	fish	–	P		
Smooth Leaf Fig	fruit	+		O	
Snails	meat	–	P		
Snake	meat	–	P		
Snake Beans	nsveg	+		M	
Snake Gourd	nsveg	+		M	
Snapper	fish	–	P		
Snow Fungus	nsveg	+		M	
Snow Peas (Mangetout/Chinese Pea)	nsveg	+		M	
Soda Bread	grains	–			S
Sole, Lemon and Dover	fish	–	P		
Sorghum	grains	–			S
Sorghum Flour	grains	–			S
Sorrel	herb	+		M	
Sourdough Bread	grains	–			S
Soured Cream*	fats/ oils	n		M	
Sow Cabbage (Jiu La Choi)	nsveg	+		M	
Sow Thistle	nsveg	+		M	

FOOD	FAMILY	+/−/n	PROTEIN	M/O	STARCH
Soya Beans*	soya	−	P		
Soya Cheese*	soya	−	P		
Soya Cream*	soya	−	P		
Soya Drink (Soya Milk)*	soya	−	P		
Soya Fibre (Okara)*	soya	−	P		
Soya Flour*	soya	−	P		
Soya Ice Cream*	soya	−	P		
Soya Lecithin*	soya	−	P		
Soya Yoghurt*	soya	−	P		
Soyabean Oil*	fats/ oils	n		M	
Spaghetti (must be egg-free)	pasta	−			S
Spaghetti Squash (Vegetable Spaghetti)	nsveg	+		M	
Spanish Melon	fruit	+		O	
Spanish Onion	nsveg	+		M	
Spearmint	herb	+		M	
Spelt	grains	−			S
Spike Rush	sveg	+			S
Spinach	nsveg	+		M	
Spinach Beet	nsveg	+		M	
Split Lentils (Red Lentils)*	pulse	−			
Split Peas*	pulse	−			
Sponge Mushroom (Morel)	nsveg	+		M	
Sprats	fish	−	P		
Spring Greens	nsveg	+		M	

FOOD	FAMILY	+/–/n	PROTEIN	M/O	STARCH
Spring Onions (Scallions/Green Onions)	nsveg	+		M	
Springroll Wrapper	grains	–			S
Sprouted Beans	nsveg	+		M	
Sprouted Seeds	nsveg	+		M	
Squash	nsveg	+		M	
Squid (Calamari)	fish	–	P		
Star Anise (Chinese Anise)*	spice	+		M	
Star Apple (Caimito)	fruit	+		O	
Star Fruit (Carambola)	fruit	+		O	
Steak and Kidney Pie (See Foods to Avoid, p.29)					
Stem Ginger (Tsee Geung)*	spice	–		M	
Stem Lettuce (Woh Sun)	nsveg	+		M	
Stinging Tree Fruit	fruit	+		O	
Strangler Fig	fruit	+		O	
Straw Mushrooms	nsveg	+		M	
Strawberries	fruit	+		O	
Suen Tau (Garlic)	herb	+		M	
Suet*	fats/ oils	–		M	
Sugar, White or Brown (See Foods to Avoid, p.29)					
Sugarsnap Peas	nsveg	+		M	
Sultanas	fruit	+		O	
Summer Grass Seeds	seeds	+		M	
Summer Orange (Valencia)	fruit	+		O	

FOOD	FAMILY	+/–/n	PROTEIN	M/O	STARCH
Sunflower Oil*	fats/ oils	n		M	
Sunflower Seeds	seeds	+		M	
Surinam Cherry (Pitagna)	fruit	+		O	
Swatow Mustard Cabbage (Daai Gaai Choi)	nsveg	+		M	
Swede (Rutabaga)	nsveg	+		M	
Sweet Chestnuts (Marron/ Lut Tzee)*	nuts	–		M	
Sweet Cicely	herb	+		M	
Sweet Lime (Limetta)	fruit	+		O	
Sweet Potato (Batata/Faan Sue)	sveg	+			S
Sweetbreads	meat	–	P		
Sweetcorn	sveg	+			S
Sweetie	fruit	+		O	
Swiss Chard (Chard)	nsveg	+		M	
Swordfish	fish	–	P		
Sze Gwa (Angled Loofah/Luffa)	nsveg	+		M	
Szechuan Pepper (Chinese Pepper)*	spice	–		M	

T ✎

Taai Goo Choi (Chinese Flat Cabbage)	nsveg	+		M	
Tagliatelle (must be egg-free)	pasta	–			S
Tahini (Sesame Seed Paste)	seeds	+		M	
Tailor	fish	–	P		

FOOD	FAMILY	+/-/n	PROTEIN	M/O	STARCH
Tamarillo (Java Plum)	fruit	+		O	
Tamarind (Indian Date)	fruit	+		O	
Tambor Seeds	seeds	+		M	
Tandoori Masala*	spice	−		M	
Tangelo (Ugli Fruit)	fruit	+		O	
Tangerines	fruit	+		O	
Tango	nsveg	+		M	
Tanjong Tree Fruit	fruit	+		O	
Tannia	sveg	+			S
Tansy	herb	+		M	
Tapioca	grains	−			S
Tarragon	herb	+		M	
Taramasalata	fish	−	P		
Taro (Eddoes/Dasheen/Kandalla)	sveg	+			S
Taro Flour	grains	+			S
Taro Leaves	nsveg	+		M	
Tasmanian Salmon	fish	−	P		
Tempeh*	soya	−	P		
Tenggiri	fish	−	P		
Teraglin	fish	−	P		
Thai Fragrant Rice (Jasmine Rice)	grains	−			S
Thistle	nsveg	+		M	
Thyme	herb	+		M	
Tiger Nuts*	nuts	−		M	
Tofu (Beancurd/Dau Foo)*	soya	−	P		

FOOD	FAMILY	+/-/n	PROTEIN	M/O	STARCH
Tomato, Cooked	nsveg	−		M	
Tomato Purée (Paste)	nsveg	−		M	
Tomato, Raw	nsveg	+		M	
Tong Ho (Garland Chrysanthemum)	nsveg	+		M	
Tongue	meat	−	P		
Torch Ginger*	spice	−		M	
Tortilla	grains	−			S
Treacle (See Foods to Avoid, p.29)					
Tree Tomato	nsveg	+		M	
Treefern Leaf	nsveg	+		M	
Trenette (must be egg-free)	pasta	−			S
Trevally	fish	−	P		
Tripe	meat	−	P		
Triticale	grains	−			S
Trombone Pumpkin	nsveg	+		M	
Trout	fish	−	P		
Truffle	nsveg	+		M	
Trumpeter	fish	−	P		
Tsee Geung (Stem Ginger)*	spice	−		M	
Tseet Gwa (Chinese Fuzzy Melon)	nsveg	+		M	
Tseng Gwa (Cucumber)	nsveg	+		M	
Tseng Jiu (Capsicums/Sweet Bell Peppers)	nsveg	+		M	
Tseng Loh Baak (Oriental Green Radish)	nsveg	+		M	

FOOD	FAMILY	+/-/n	PROTEIN	M/O	STARCH
Ts'ung Tau (Shallots)	nsveg	+		M	
Tuna	fish	–	P		
Turbot	fish	–	P		
Turkey	meat	–	P		
Turmeric*	spice	–		M	
Turnip Greens	nsveg	+		M	
Turnips	nsveg	+		M	
Turtle Bean (Black Kidney Bean)*	pulse	–			
Turtle Eggs	eggs/ dairy	–	P		
TVP – Textured Vegetable Protein*	soya	–	P		

U ∾

FOOD	FAMILY	+/-/n	PROTEIN	M/O	STARCH
Uen Sai (Cilantro/Coriander)	herb	+		M	
Ugli Fruit (Tangelo)	fruit	+		O	
UHT Milk	eggs/ dairy	–	P		
Umbrella Bush Seeds	seeds	+		M	
Umeboshi Plum	fruit	+		O	

V ∾

FOOD	FAMILY	+/-/n	PROTEIN	M/O	STARCH
Valencia Orange (Summer Orange)	fruit	+		O	
Vanaspati (Vegetable Ghee)*	fats/ oils	n		M	

FOOD	FAMILY	+/–/n	PROTEIN	M/O	STARCH
Veal	meat	–	P		
Vegetable Ghee (Vanaspati)*	fats/oils	n		M	
Vegetable Pear (Chayote/Choko/Cho Cho/Hop Jeung Gwa)	nsveg	+		M	
Vegetable Oil*	fats/oils	n		M	
Vegetable Spaghetti (Spaghetti Squash)	nsveg	+		M	
Venison	meat	–	P		
Vermicelli (Capellini – must be egg-free)	pasta	–			S
Vinegar*	condiment	–		M	
Vine Leaf	nsveg	+		M	

W

FOOD	FAMILY	+/–/n	PROTEIN	M/O	STARCH
Wakame	nsveg	+		M	
Walnut Oil*	fats/oils	n		M	
Walnuts*	nuts	–		M	
Wan Yee (Jew's Ear Mushrooms)	nsveg	+		M	
Warrigal Greens	nsveg	+		M	
Water Chestnut (Link Gok)	nsveg	+		M	
Water Lily Seeds	seeds	+		M	
Water Melon	fruit	+		O	

FOOD	FAMILY	+/-/n	PROTEIN	M/O	STARCH
Water Spinach (Kang Kong/ Ong Choi)	nsveg	+		M	
Watercress (Sai Yeung Choi)	nsveg	+		M	
Waxgourd (Winter Melon/ Dong Gwa)	nsveg	+		M	
Webbs Lettuce	nsveg	+		M	
West Indian Pea	nsveg	+		M	
Wheat	grains	–			S
Wheat Noodles (Noodles —must be egg-free)	pasta	–			S
Wheatgerm	grains	–			S
Wheatgerm Oil*	fats/ oils	n		M	
Whelks	fish	–	P		
Whey	eggs/ dairy	+	P		
White Aspen Fruit	fruit	+		O	
White Bread	grains	–			S
White Cabbage	nsveg	+		M	
White Pepper*	condi- ment	–		M	
White Pomfret	fish	–	P		
White Rice	grains	–			S
White Sweet Potato	sveg	+			S
White Wormwood (Junn Jiu Choi)	nsveg	+		M	
Whitebait	fish	–	P		
Whitecurrants	fruit	+		O	
Whiting	fish	–	P		

FOOD	FAMILY	+/-/n	PROTEIN	M/O	STARCH
Whole Dried Pea (Blue Pea)*	pulse	–			
Wholemeal Bread	grains	–			S
Wholemeal Flour	grains	–			S
Wholemeal Pasta (Brown Pasta — must be egg-free)	pasta	–			S
Wild Boar	meat	–	P		
Wild Fig	fruit	+		O	
Wild Ginger	fruit	+		O	
Wild Grape	fruit	+		O	
Wild Onion	nsveg	+		M	
Wild Orange (Native Capers)	fruit	+		O	
Wild Parsnip	nsveg	+		M	
Wild Raspberries	fruit	+		O	
Wild Rice	grains	–			S
Wild Rice Shoots (Gaau Sun)	herb	+		M	
Windsor Black Pumpkin	nsveg	+		M	
Wine Vinegar*	condi-ment	–		M	
Winged Pea/Bean (Asparagus Pea/Four Angled Bean)	nsveg	+		M	
Winkles	fish	–	P		
Winter Melon (Waxgourd/ Dong Gwa)	nsveg	+		M	
Winter Mushrooms (Shiitaki/ Dong Gwoo)	nsveg	+		M	
Winter Orange (Navel/Seville Orange)	fruit	+		O	

FOOD	FAMILY	+/-/n	PROTEIN	M/O	STARCH
Witchetty Bush Seeds	seeds	+		M	
Witchetty Grubs	meat	–	P		
Woh Sun (Stem Lettuce)	nsveg	+		M	
Wong Gwa (Yellow Cucumber)	nsveg	+		M	
Wongi Plum	fruit	+		O	
Woodruff	herb	+		M	
Woolybutt Grass Seeds	seeds	+		M	
Worcestershire Sauce*	condiment	–		M	
Wrasse	fish	–	P		

Y

FOOD	FAMILY	+/-/n	PROTEIN	M/O	STARCH
Yam (Shu Yu)	sveg	+			S
Yam Bean (Jicama/Sha Ge)	sveg	+			S
Yam Flour	grains	–			S
Yard-Long Bean (Asparagus Bean)	nsveg	+		M	
Yarrow	herb	+		M	
Ye Choi Fa (Cauliflower)	nsveg	+		M	
Yeast Extract (See Foods to Avoid, p.29)					
Yeh Choi (Head Cabbage)	nsveg	+		M	
Yellow Apricots	fruit	+		O	
Yellow Cucumber (Wong Gwa)	nsveg	+		M	
Yellow Mushroom (Boletus)	nsveg	+		M	
Yellow Walnut*	nuts	–		M	
Yellowfin Tuna	fish	–	P		

FOOD	FAMILY	+/-/n	PROTEIN	M/O	STARCH
Yin Choi (Chinese Spinach)	nsveg	+		M	
Yoghurt	eggs/dairy	+	P		
Yun Meen (Dracontomelun)	fruit	+		O	

Z ∾

Zeitan (Seitan)	grains	−			S
Zucchini (Courgette)	nsveg	+		M	

Food Families

⌒

```
*  = In moderation only
+  = Alkaline-forming
−  = Acid-forming
n  = Neither
P  = Protein
M  = Mix with anything
O  = Eat on its own
S  = Starch
```

FOOD	+/-/n	PROTEIN	M/O	STARCH

Fruit

Treat all fruit as alkaline-forming. For most people fruit is likely to be better digested and its energy-packed nutrients absorbed more efficiently if you eat it separately from proteins and starches. See page 20 for more information.

FOOD	+/-/n	PROTEIN	M/O	STARCH
Abiu	+		O	
African Horned Melon (Kiwano)	+		O	
Alpine Strawberry	+		O	
Amia	+		O	
Apple Juice	+		O	
Apple-Berry	+		O	
Apples	+		O	
Apricot Fig	+		O	
Apricots	+		O	
Asian Breadfruit	+		O	
Asian Pear (Nashi)	+		O	
Awalyuru	+		O	
Babaco (Babacao)	+		O	
Banana	+		O	
Ber (Chinese Apple/Indian Jujube Plum)	+		O	
Billabong Tree Fruit	+		O	
Billy Goat Plum	+		O	
Black Apple	+		O	

FOOD	+/-/n	PROTEIN	M/O	STARCH
Black Cherries	+		O	
Black Olives	+		O	
Black Sapote (Chocolate Pudding Fruit)	+		O	
Blackberries	+		O	
Blackcurrants	+		O	
Blood Orange	+		O	
Blue Quandong Fruit	+		O	
Blueberries	+		O	
Boysenberries	+		O	
Brazilian Tree Grape (Jaboticaba)	+		O	
Bullocks Heart Custard Apple	+		O	
Burdekin Plum	+		O	
Bush Banana	+		O	
Bush Lemon	+		O	
Bush Passionfruit	+		O	
Bush Plum	+		O	
Bush Raisin	+		O	
Bush Tomato	+		O	
Cactus Fruit (Prickly Pear/Indian Fig)	+		O	
Caimito (Star Apple)	+		O	
Canistel (Egg Fruit/Marmalade Fruit)	+		O	
Cantaloup Melon	+		O	
Cape Gooseberry (Physalis)	+		O	
Carambola (Star Fruit)	+		O	
Casaba Melon	+		O	

FOOD	+/-/n	PROTEIN M/O	STARCH
Cashew Fruit	+	O	
Cassowary Gum Fruit	+	O	
Cedar Bay Cherry	+	O	
Charentais Melon	+	O	
Cheese Fruit	+	O	
Cherimoya Custard Apple	+	O	
Cherries	+	O	
Cherries (glacé)	–		S
Cherry Plums	+	O	
Chinese Apple (Ber/Indian Jujube Plum)	+	O	
Chinese Gooseberry (Kiwi Fruit)	+	O	
Chinese Red Date	+	O	
Chocolate Pudding Fruit (Black Sapote)	+	O	
Christmas Melon (Santa Claus Melon)	+	O	
Citron	+	O	
Citronen (German Lemon)	+	O	
Clementines	+	O	
Cloudberry	+	O	
Cocky Apple	+	O	
Conkerberry Fruit	+	O	
Crab Apple	+	O	
Cranberries	+	O	
Crater Aspen Fruit	+	O	
Crenshaw Melon	+	O	
Cumquat (Kumquat)	+	O	

FOOD	+/−/n	PROTEIN	M/O	STARCH
Currant Bush Fruit	+		O	
Currants	+		O	
Custard Apple	+		O	
Dabugay	+		O	
Damson	+		O	
Date Plum (Persimmon/Kaki Fruit/ Sharon Fruit)	+		O	
Davidson Plum	+		O	
Dodder Laurel Fruit	+		O	
Dracontomelun (Yun Meen)	+		O	
Dried Apple	+		O	
Dried Apricot	+		O	
Dried Banana	+		O	
Dried Fig	+		O	
Dried Fruits (all kinds)	+		O	
Dried Nectarine	+		O	
Dried Peach	+		O	
Dried Pear	+		O	
Durian	+		O	
Elderberry	+		O	
Emu Berry	+		O	
Feijoa (Pineapple Guava)	+		O	
Figs	+		O	
Finger Lime	+		O	
Fruit Juices (all types)	+		O	
Galia Melon	+		O	

FOOD	+/-/n	PROTEIN	M/O	STARCH
Geebung	+		O	
Gooseberries	+		O	
Granadillas (Passion Fruit)	+		O	
Grape Juice	+		O	
Grapefruit	+		O	
Grapefruit Juice	+		O	
Grapes (all types)	+		O	
Green Ginger Fruit	+		O	
Green Olives	+		O	
Green Plum	+		O	
Greengages	+		O	
Guava	+		O	
Honeydew Melon	+		O	
Horned Melon (Kiwano)	+		O	
Huckleberries	+		O	
Hunza Apricots	+		O	
Indian Date (Tamarind)	+		O	
Indian Fig (Cactus Fruit/Prickly Pear)	+		O	
Indian Jujube Plum (Ber/Chinese Apple)	+		O	
Jaboticaba (Brazilian Tree Grape)	+		O	
Jackfruit	+		O	
Jambu Fruit	+		O	
Java Plum (Tamarillo)	+		O	
Juniper Berries	+		O	
Jurdal	+		O	

FOOD	+/-/n	PROTEIN	M/O	STARCH
Kalamansi	+		0	
Kiwano Melon (Horned Melon)	+		0	
Kiwi Fruit (Chinese Gooseberry)	+		0	
Kumquat (Cumquat)	+		0	
Lavan Melon	+		0	
Lawyer Vine Fruit	+		0	
Lemon Juice	+		0	
Lemons	+		0	
Lillypilly Fruits	+		0	
Lime Juice	+		0	
Limes	+		0	
Limetta (Sweet Lime)	+		0	
Loganberries	+		0	
Longans	+		0	
Loquat (Japanese Medlar)	+		0	
Lychees	+		0	
Malaga Bean Fruit	+		0	
Mammie Apple	+		0	
Mandarins	+		0	
Mango Juice	+		0	
Mangos	+		0	
Mangosteen	+		0	
Medlars	+		0	
Melons (all types)	+		0	
Midjin	+		0	

FOOD	+/-/n	PROTEIN	M/O	STARCH
Mixed Peel (can be mixed in small amounts with starch)	+		O	
Mongo	+		O	
Mulberries	+		O	
Narrow-Leaf Bumble	+		O	
Nashi (Asian Pear)	+		O	
Native Banana	+		O	
Native Capers (Wild Orange)	+		O	
Native Cucumber Fruit	+		O	
Native Grape	+		O	
Native Guava	+		O	
Native Melon	+		O	
Navel Orange (Winter/Seville Orange)	+		O	
Nectarines	+		O	
Nipan	+		O	
Nonda Plum	+		O	
Nypa Palm Fruit	+		O	
Ogen Melon	+		O	
Olives (all types)	+		O	
Orange Juice	+		O	
Oranges	+		O	
Ortaniques	+		O	
Pandanus	+		O	
Papaya (Paw-Paw)	+		O	
Passion Fruit (Granadillas)	+		O	
Passion Fruit Juice	+		O	

FOOD	+/-/o	PROTEIN	M/O	STARCH
Paw-Paw (Papaya)	+		o	
Peaches	+		o	
Pears	+		o	
Pepino	+		o	
Persian Melon	+		o	
Persimmon (Date Plum/Kaki Fruit)	+		o	
Physalis (Cape Gooseberry)	+		o	
Pigface Fruit	+		o	
Pineapple	+		o	
Pineapple Guava (Feijoa)	+		o	
Pineapple Juice	+		o	
Pitagna (Surinam Cherry)	+		o	
Plantain	+		o	
Pluster Fig	+		o	
Pomegranate	+		o	
Pomelo (Shaddock)	+		o	
Prickly Pear (Cactus Fruit/Indian Fig)	+		o	
Prune	+		o	
Prune Juice	+		o	
Quince	+		o	
Regah	+		o	
Raisins	+		o	
Rambutan	+		o	
Raspberries	+		o	
Redcurrants	+		o	

FOOD	+/-/n	PROTEIN	M/O	STARCH
Rock Melon	+		O	
Rose Hips	+		O	
Ruby Saltbush Fruit	+		O	
Sandpaper Fig	+		O	
Santa Claus Melon (Christmas Melon)	+		O	
Sapodilla	+		O	
Satsumas	+		O	
Seville Orange (Winter/Navel Orange)	+		O	
Shaddock (Pomelo)	+		O	
Sharon Fruit (Persimmon)	+		O	
Smooth Leaf Fig	+		O	
Spanish Melon	+		O	
Star Apple (Caimito)	+		O	
Star Fruit (Carambola)	+		O	
Stinging Tree Fruit	+		O	
Strangler Fig	+		O	
Strawberries	+		O	
Sultanas	+		O	
Surinam Cherry (Pitagna)	+		O	
Sweet Lime (Limetta)	+		O	
Sweetie	+		O	
Tamarillo (Java Plum)	+		O	
Tamarind (Indian Date)	+		O	
Tangelo (Ugli Fruit)	+		O	
Tangerines	+		O	

FOOD	+/-/n	PROTEIN	M/O	STARCH
Tanjong Tree Fruit	+		O	
Ugli Fruit (Tangelo)	+		O	
Umeboshi Plum	+		O	
Valencia Orange (Summer Orange)	+		O	
Water Melon	+		O	
White Aspen Fruit	+		O	
Whitecurrants	+		O	
Wild Fig	+		O	
Wild Ginger	+		O	
Wild Grape	+		O	
Wild Orange (Native Capers)	+		O	
Wild Raspberries	+		O	
Wongi Plum	+		O	
Yellow Apricots	+		O	

Non-Starchy Vegetables and Salad Foods (mix with anything) ❧

These versatile vegetables are all classed as 'mix-with-anything' foods and, with the exception of asparagus, are alkaline-forming.

Acorn Squash	+		M	
Agar (gelling agent from seaweed)	+		M	
Alfalfa Sprouts	+		M	
America Cress (Land Cress)	+		M	

FOOD	+/-/n	PROTEIN	M/O	STARCH
Angled Loofah or Luffa (Sze Gwa)	+		M	
Apple Cucumber	+		M	
Arame (seaweed)	+		M	
Arrowhead Tubers (Chi Gu)	+		M	
Artichokes	+		M	
Asparagus	−		M	
Asparagus Bean (Yard-Long Bean)	+		M	
Asparagus Pea (Winged Bean/Four Angled Bean/Winged Pea)	+		M	
Aubergine (Eggplant/Brinjal/Aigwa)	+		M	
Australian Cranesbill	+		M	
Avocado (Alligator Pear)	+		M	
Baby Blue Pumpkin	+		M	
Baby Squash (Patty Pan)	+		M	
Bamboo Fungus	+		M	
Bamboo Mustard Cabbage (Chuk Gaai Choi)	+		M	
Bamboo Shoots (Chuk Sun)	+		M	
Banana Pumpkin	+		M	
Bean Sprouts (Dau Nga Choi)	+		M	
Beet Greens	+		M	
Beetroot	+		M	
Belgian Endive (Chicory)	+		M	
Bitter Gourd (Bitter Melon/Foo Gwa)	+		M	
Blanched Chinese Chives (Gau Wong)	+		M	
Blue Max Pumpkin	+		M	

FOOD	+/-/n	PROTEIN	M/O	STARCH
Bok Choi (Chinese White Cabbage)	+		M	
Boletus (Yellow Mushroom)	+		M	
Bottle Gourd	+		M	
Bracken Root	+		M	
Bracken Tip	+		M	
Brinjal (Aubergine/Eggplant/Aigwa)	+		M	
Broad Beans (fresh)	+		M	
Broadleaf Batavian Endive (Escarole)	+		M	
Broccoflower	+		M	
Broccoli	+		M	
Brown Mushroom	+		M	
Brussels Sprouts	+		M	
Burdock Root	+		M	
Burnet	+		M	
Butter Pumpkin	+		M	
Butterhead Lettuce	+		M	
Butternut Pumpkin	+		M	
Button Mushroom	+		M	
Button Onion	+		M	
Cabbage — Red, Green or White	+		M	
Cabbage Tree Palm	+		M	
Calabrese (Green-Headed Broccoli)	+		M	
Capsicums (Peppers, Tseng Jiu)	+		M	
Carragheen	+		M	
Carrots	+		M	

FOOD	+/-/n	PROTEIN	M/O	STARCH
Cattle Pumpkin	+		M	
Cauliflower (Ye Choi Fa)	+		M	
Celeriac	+		M	
Celery (Kunn Choi)	+		M	
Celery Cabbage	+		M	
Celery Flowering Cabbage	+		M	
Cep Mushroom (Cepes)	+		M	
Chanterelle (Egg Mushroom)	+		M	
Chard (Swiss Chard)	+		M	
Chayote (Cho Cho, Choko, Vegetable Pear, Hop Jeung Gwa)	+		M	
Chekur Manis	+		M	
Chilli Peppers	+		M	
Chinese Arrowhead Leaves	+		M	
Chinese Black Moss	+		M	
Chinese Boxthorn (Gau Gei Choi)	+		M	
Chinese Broccoli	+		M	
Chinese Cabbage	+		M	
Chinese Chives Flowers (Gau Choi Fa)	+		M	
Chinese Flat Cabbage (Taai Goo Choi)	+		M	
Chinese Flowering Cabbage (Choi Sam)	+		M	
Chinese Fuzzy Melon (Tseet Gwa)	+		M	
Chinese Kale (Gaai Laan)	+		M	
Chinese Long Beans (Dau Gok)	+		M	
Chinese Mushrooms (Oyster Mushrooms/ Pleurotte)	+		M	

FOOD	+/-/n	PROTEIN	M/O	STARCH
Chinese Mustard (Mustard Cabbage/ Kai Choi)	+		M	
Chinese Pea (Mangetout/Snow Peas)	+		M	
Chinese Radish	+		M	
Chinese Spinach (Yin Choi)	+		M	
Chinese Water Chestnut	+		M	
Chinese Water Cabbage (Bok Choi)	+		M	
Cho Cho (Choko/Chayote/Hop Jeung Gwa)	+		M	
Cloud Ear Fungus	+		M	
Cole Leaves	+		M	
Collard (Kale/Borecole)	+		M	
Cong Dou (Petah)	+		M	
Cos Lettuce (Romaine)	+		M	
Courgette (Zucchini)	+		M	
Cowpea (Fresh Pods)	+		M	
Cress	+		M	
Crisphead Lettuce	+		M	
Crown Prince Pumpkin	+		M	
Cucumber (Tseng Gwa)	+		M	
Curly Endive	+		M	
Curly Kale	+		M	
Cycad	+		M	
Daikon (Oriental White Radish/Loh Baak)	+		M	
Dandelion Leaves	+		M	
Daun Salam	+		M	

FOOD	+/-/n	PROTEIN	M/O	STARCH
Drumstick Leaves	+		M	
Drumstick Vegetable	+		M	
Dudi	+		M	
Dulse	+		M	
Egg Mushroom (Chanterelle)	+		M	
Eggplant (Aubergine/Aigwa/Brinjal)	+		M	
Endive	+		M	
Enoki Mushroom	+		M	
Enorkitake Mushroom	+		M	
Escarole (Broadleaf Batavian Endive)	+		M	
Field Mushroom	+		M	
Fenugreek Sprouts	+		M	
Four Angled Bean (Winged Bean/ Winged Pea/Asparagus Pea)	+		M	
French Beans	+		M	
Fungi	+		M	
Garland Chrysanthemum (Tong Ho)	+		M	
Gherkin Cucumber (fresh only, not pickled)	+		M	
Globe Artichoke	+		M	
Golden Nugget Pumpkin	+		M	
Good King Henry (Poor Man's Asparagus)	+		M	
Gourd	+		M	
Green-Headed Cauliflower (Romanesco)	+		M	
Green Onions (Scallions/Spring Onions)	+		M	
Head Cabbage (Yeh Choi)	+		M	
Hijiki	+		M	

FOOD	+/-/n	PROTEIN	M/O	STARCH
Hubbard Pumpkin (Hubbard Squash)	+		M	
Iceberg Lettuce	+		M	
Jarrahdale Pumpkin	+		M	
Jerusalem Artichoke	+		M	
Jew's Ear Mushrooms (Wan Yee)	+		M	
Kale (Collard/Borecole)	+		M	
Kang Kong (Water Spinach/Ong Choi)	+		M	
Kelp	+		M	
Kohlrabi (Gaai Laan Tau)	+		M	
Kombu	+		M	
Kuichai Onion	+		M	
Lamb's Lettuce (Mache/Corn Salad)	+		M	
Land Cress (America Cress)	+		M	
Laver (Nori/Sloke/Slake)	+		M	
Leaf Lettuce	+		M	
Leek (Daai Suen)	+		M	
Lemon Grass	+		M	
Lettuce (all types)	+		M	
Lollo Rosso	+		M	
Lotus Tubers (Leen Ngau)	+		M	
Mache (Lamb's Lettuce/Corn Salad)	+		M	
Mangetout (Snow Peas/Chinese Pea)	+		M	
Marrow	+		M	
Matsutake Mushrooms	+		M	
Mekabu	+		M	

FOOD	+/-/n	PROTEIN	M/O	STARCH
Morel (Sponge Mushroom)	+		M	
Mushrooms	+		M	
Mustard & Cress	+		M	
Mustard Cabbage (Chinese Mustard/ Kai Choi)	+		M	
Mustard Greens	+		M	
Nameko	+		M	
Nasturtium	+		M	
Native Onion	+		M	
Nettles	+		M	
New Zealand Spinach	+		M	
Nori (Laver/Sloke/Slake)	+		M	
Oakleaf Lettuce	+		M	
Oarweed	+		M	
Okra (Ladies' Fingers/Gumbo)	+		M	
Onion	+		M	
Oriental Green Radish (Tseng Loh Baak)	+		M	
Oriental White Radish (Daikon/Loh Baak)	+		M	
Oyster Mushroom (Chinese Mushroom/ Pleurotte)	+		M	
Oyster Plant (Salsify)	+		M	
Pak Choi Cabbage	+		M	
Palm Heart	+		M	
Parakeelya Leaves	+		M	
Parasole Mushroom	+		M	
Parsnips	+		M	

FOOD	+/-/n	PROTEIN	M/O	STARCH
Patra Leaves	+		M	
Patty Pan (Baby Squash)	+		M	
Pea Shoots (Dau Miu)	+		M	
Peas (fresh)	+		M	
Peking Cabbage (Napa)	+		M	
Petah (Cong Dou)	+		M	
Petit Pois	+		M	
Pigface Leaves	+		M	
Pointed Head Cabbage	+		M	
Porcini (Wild Mushroom)	+		M	
Puff Ball	+		M	
Pumpkin	+		M	
Purple Sprouting Broccoli	+		M	
Queensland Blue Pumpkin	+		M	
Radicchio Chicory	+		M	
Radishes, White and Red	+		M	
Red Cabbage	+		M	
Red Onions	+		M	
Reishi Mushroom	+		M	
Rocket (Arugula)	+		M	
Romaine Lettuce (Cos)	+		M	
Romanesco (Green-Headed Cauliflower)	+		M	
Runner Beans	+		M	
Rutabaga (Swede)	+		M	
Salsify (Oyster Plant)	+		M	

FOOD	+/-ln	PROTEIN	M/O	STARCH
Samphire	+		M	
Sand Palm	+		M	
Sauerkraut	+		M	
Savoy Cabbage	+		M	
Scallions (Spring/Green Onions)	+		M	
Screw Pine	+		M	
Sea Kale	+		M	
Sea Lettuce	+		M	
Sea Parsley (Lovage)	+		M	
Seaweed (all types)	+		M	
Shallots (Ts'ung Tau)	+		M	
Shiitaki (Winter Mushrooms/Dong Gwoo)	+		M	
Silama Spinach	+		M	
Silverbeet	+		M	
Slippery Vegetable Leaves (Saan Choi)	+		M	
Sloke (Slake/Nori/Laver)	+		M	
Snake Beans	+		M	
Snake Gourd	+		M	
Snow Fungus	+		M	
Snow Peas (Mangetout/Chinese Pea)	+		M	
Sow Cabbage (Jiu La Choi)	+		M	
Sow Thistle	+		M	
Spaghetti Squash (Vegetable Spaghetti)	+		M	
Spanish Onion	+		M	
Spinach	+		M	

FOOD	+/-/n	PROTEIN	M/O	STARCH
Spinach Beet	+		M	
Sponge Mushroom (Morel)	+		M	
Spring Greens	+		M	
Spring Onions (Scallions/Green Onions)	+		M	
Sprouted Beans	+		M	
Sprouted Seeds	+		M	
Squash	+		M	
Stem Lettuce (Woh Sun)	+		M	
Straw Mushrooms	+		M	
Sugarsnap Peas	+		M	
Swatow Mustard Cabbage (Daai Gaai Choi)	+		M	
Swede (Rutabaga)	+		M	
Swiss Chard (Chard)	+		M	
Tango	+		M	
Taro Leaves	+		M	
Thistle	+		M	
Tomato, Cooked	–		M	
Tomato Purée (Paste)	–		M	
Tomato, Raw	+		M	
Tree Tomato	+		M	
Treefern Leaf	+		M	
Trombone Pumpkin	+		M	
Truffle	+		M	
Turnip Greens	+		M	
Turnips	+		M	

FOOD	+/-/n	PROTEIN	M/O	STARCH
Vegetable Spaghetti (Spaghetti Squash)	+		M	
Vine Leaf	+		M	
Wakame	+		M	
Warrigal Greens	+		M	
Water Chestnut (Link Gok)	+		M	
Water Spinach (Kang Kong/Ong Choi)	+		M	
Watercress (Sai Yeung Choi)	+		M	
Waxgourd (Winter Melon/Dong Gwa)	+		M	
Webbs Lettuce	+		M	
West Indian Pea	+		M	
White Cabbage	+		M	
White Wormwood (Junn Jiu Choi)	+		M	
Wild Onion	+		M	
Wild Parsnip	+		M	
Windsor Black Pumpkin	+		M	
Winged Bean (Four Angled Bean/ Winged Pea/Asparagus Pea)	+		M	
Winged Pea (Four Angled Bean/ Winged Bean/Asparagus Pea)	+		M	
Winter Melon (Waxgourd/Dong Gwa)	+		M	
Yellow Cucumber (Wong Gwa)	+		M	
Yellow Mushroom (Boletus)	+		M	
Zucchini (Courgette)	+		M	

Herbs and Spices 〜

Herbs and spices are versatile additions which mix
happily with proteins, starches, salads and all kinds of
vegetables. Some herbs (e.g. dandelion and nettle) are
also used as vegetables. Others (for example, fenugreek
and mustard) produce seeds which, when ground, are
classed as spices. For this reason, some botanicals may
appear in more than one category in the food lists. Be
adventurous with fresh culinary herbs: they are packed
with nutrients. But be sparing with spices: they provide
additional flavouring and nourishment in many dishes
but can aggravate digestive disorders if taken in large
amounts.

Important safety note: Many herbs and spices also have
medicinal properties and should never be taken in large
quantities. Indeed, when using them as therapeutic
medicines, it is wise to obtain the professional guidance
of a qualified herbalist.

FOOD	+/-/n	PROTEIN M/O	STARCH
Aamchur (Amchoor/Mango Powder)*	–	M	
Ajwain*	–	M	
Alexanders (Black Lovage/Horse Parsley)	+	M	
Allspice*	–	M	
Angelica	+	M	
Anise (Aniseed)	+	M	
Basil	+	M	
Bay Leaf	+	M	

FOOD	+/-/n	PROTEIN	M/O	STARCH
Bergamot (Bee Balm/Red Bergamot)	+		M	
Betel Leaves	+		M	
Black Pepper (See Condiments)	−		M	
Borage	+		M	
Capers*	−		M	
Cardamom*	−		M	
Cassia (Bastard Cinnamon)*	−		M	
Cayenne (Chilli)*	+		M	
Chaat Masala*	−		M	
Chamomile	+		M	
Chervil	+		M	
Chilli (Cayenne)*	+		M	
Chinese Chives (Garlic Chives/Gau Choi)	+		M	
Chinese Key*	+		M	
Chinese Pepper (Szechuan Pepper)*	−		M	
Chinese 5 Spice*	−		M	
Chives	+		M	
Cilantro (Coriander/Uen Sai)	+		M	
Cinnamon*	−		M	
Cloves*	−		M	
Comfrey	+		M	
Coriander (Cilantro/Uen Sai)	+		M	
Cumin (ground)*	−		M	
Curry Leaf	+		M	
Curry Powder*	−		M	

FOOD	+/-/n	PROTEIN	M/O	STARCH
Dandelion	+		M	
Dhansak Masala*	−		M	
Dill	+		M	
Elderflower	+		M	
Fennel Leaves	+		M	
Fennel (ground seeds)*	+		M	
Fenugreek (ground seeds)*	+		M	
Galangal*	−		M	
Garam Masala*	−		M	
Garlic (Suan Tau)	+		M	
Ginger, fresh stem (Tsee Geung)*	−		M	
Ginger, ground (Geung)*	−		M	
Gomasio (Sesame Salt) (See Condiments)*	−		M	
Hops	+		M	
Horseradish*	−		M	
Hyssop	+		M	
Indian Borage	+		M	
Juniper	+		M	
Kashmiri Masala*	−		M	
Ketumbar Jawa	−		M	
Laksa	−		M	
Lemon Balm	+		M	
Lemon Grass	+		M	
Lemon Thyme	+		M	
Lemon Verbena	+		M	

FOOD	+/-/n	PROTEIN	M/O	STARCH
Lime Flowers	+		M	
Lime Leaves (Daun Limau Perut)	+		M	
Liquorice*	–		M	
Lovage (Sea Parsley)	+		M	
Mace*	–		M	
Mahlab*	–		M	
Marjoram	+		M	
Mint	+		M	
Mixed Spice*	–		M	
Mustard* (ground)	–		M	
Myrtle	+		M	
Nettle	+		M	
Nutmeg*	–		M	
Oregano	+		M	
Paprika*	–		M	
Parsley	+		M	
Penny Royal	+		M	
Peppermint	+		M	
Purslane	+		M	
Rosemary	+		M	
Saffron*	–		M	
Sage	+		M	
Salad Burnet	+		M	
Sambar Masala*	–		M	
Sansho Powder*	–		M	

FOOD	+/-/n	PROTEIN	M/O	STARCH
Savory	+		M	
Shiso	+		M	
Sorrel	+		M	
Spearmint	+		M	
Star Anise (Chinese Anise)*	+		M	
Stem Ginger (Tsee Geung)*	−		M	
Sweet Cicely	+		M	
Tandoori Masala*	−		M	
Tansy	+		M	
Tarragon	+		M	
Thyme	+		M	
Torch Ginger*	−		M	
Turmeric*	−		M	
Wild Rice Shoots (Gaau Sun)	+		M	
Woodruff	+		M	
Yarrow	+		M	

Seeds (mix with anything) ∾

All seeds are listed in *The Food Combiner's Meal Planner* as 'mix-with-anything' foods and all are alkaline-forming. Avoid toasted seeds. The oils they contain can be damaged easily by heating. If you want to include seeds in hot meals, add them after the cooking process is completed, just before serving.

FOOD	+/-/n	PROTEIN M/O	STARCH
Amaranth Seeds	+	M	
Anise Seeds (Aniseed)	+	M	
Black Onion Seeds (Kalonji/Nigella)	+	M	
Boab Seeds	+	M	
Breadnut Seeds	+	M	
Caraway Seeds	+	M	
Celery Seeds	+	M	
Colony Wattle Seeds	+	M	
Desert Acacia Seeds	+	M	
Dill Seeds	+	M	
Flame Tree Seeds	+	M	
Fringe Rush Seeds	+	M	
Gundabluey Seeds	+	M	
Linseeds	+	M	
Lotus Seeds	+	M	
Melon Seeds	+	M	
Mulga Seeds	+	M	
Mustard Seeds	+	M	
Native Millet	+	M	
Nigella (Black Onion Seeds/Kalonji)	+	M	
Northern Kurrajong Seeds	+	M	
Parakeelya Seeds	+	M	
Pepitas (Pumpkin Seeds)	+	M	
Poppy Seeds	+	M	
Pumpkin Seeds (Pepitas)	+	M	

FOOD	+/-/n	PROTEIN	M/O	STARCH
Red Flowered Kurrajong Seeds	+		M	
Saw Sedge Seeds	+		M	
Sesame Seed Paste (Tahini)	+		M	
Sesame Seeds	+		M	
Summer Grass Seeds	+		M	
Sunflower Seeds	+		M	
Tahini (Sesame Seed Paste)	+		M	
Tambor Seeds	+		M	
Umbrella Bush Seeds	+		M	
Water Lily Seeds	+		M	
Witchetty Bush Seeds	+		M	
Woolybutt Grass Seeds	+		M	

Nuts ∾

Use nuts in moderation only. They can be mixed in small amounts with proteins or starches; all are acid-forming apart from almonds and brazils. Keep roasted nuts to a minimum. Also, remember that peanuts are not nuts but pulses. You'll find more information about nuts on page 168.

Almonds*	+		M	
Baby Coconut*	–		M	
Barcelona Nuts*	–		M	
Betel Nuts (Areca)*	–		M	

FOOD	+/-/n	PROTEIN	M/O	STARCH
Bitter Almonds*	–		M	
Bottle Tree Nuts*	–		M	
Brazil Nuts*	+		M	
Bunya Bunya Pine Nuts*	–		M	
Bush Nuts*	–		M	
Butter Nut*	–		M	
Candle Nuts*	–		M	
Cashew Nuts*	–		M	
Coconut*	–		M	
Coconut, desiccated*	–		M	
Filberts (Hazelnuts)*	–		M	
Ginkgo Nuts*	–		M	
Ground Almonds*	–		M	
Hazelnuts (Filberts)*	–		M	
Indian Almonds*	–		M	
Johnstone River Almonds*	–		M	
Kurrajong*	–		M	
Macadamia Nuts (Queensland Nuts)*	–		M	
Macapuno*	–		M	
Marron (Sweet Chestnuts/Lut Tzee)*	–		M	
Nutbush Nuts*	–		M	
Palm Nuts*	–		M	
Pandanus Nuts*	–		M	
Pecan Nuts*	–		M	
Pesto (pesto sauce)*	–		M	

FOOD	+/-/n	PROTEIN	M/O	STARCH
Pine Nuts (Pine Kernels)*	–		M	
Pistachios*	–		M	
Quandong*	–		M	
Queensland Nuts (Macadamia Nuts)*	–		M	
Red Bopple Nuts*	–		M	
Sandalwood Nuts*	–		M	
Sweet Chestnuts (Marron/Lut Tzee)*	–		M	
Tiger Nuts*	–		M	
Walnuts*	–		M	
Water Chestnuts (Link Gok) (See Non-Starchy Vegetables)				
Yellow Walnut*	–		M	

Meat, Poultry and Game (all acid-forming proteins) ∾

All foods under this heading are acid-forming proteins. They mix well with all non-starchy vegetables, salads, seeds and herbs but not with starch or starchy vegetables. Choose free-range/organic cuts wherever possible.

Aspic	–	P	
Bacon (organic, free-range only)*	–	P	
Beef (all cuts, but organic free-range only)	–	P	
Beef Sausages*	–	P	

FOOD	+/-/n	PROTEIN	M/O	STARCH
Beefburgers*	−	P		
Brains	−	P		
Buffalo	−	P		
Calf's Liver	−	P		
Chicken (free-range only)	−	P		
Chops (all types)	−	P		
Duck	−	P		
Fillet Steak (beef)	−	P		
Frog's Legs	−	P		
Gammon	−	P		
Gelatin	−	P		
Goanna	−	P		
Goose	−	P		
Grouse	−	P		
Guinea Fowl	−	P		
Ham (organic, free-range)*	−	P		
Hare	−	P		
Heart	−	P		
Kidney	−	P		
Lamb (all cuts)	−	P		
Lamb's Kidney	−	P		
Lamb's Liver	−	P		
Lights	−	P		
Liver	−	P		
Lizard	−	P		

FOOD	+/-/n	PROTEIN	M/O	STARCH
Mutton	–	P		
Offal	–	P		
Ox Tail	–	P		
Partridge	–	P		
Pâté, Meat	–	P		
Pheasant	–	P		
Pigeon	–	P		
Pig's Trotters (organic, free-range)*	–	P		
Pork (all cuts; organic, free-range)*	–	P		
Pork Sausages (starch-free; organic, free-range)*	–	P		
Quail	–	P		
Rabbit	–	P		
Rump Steak (beef)	–	P		
Salami	–	P		
Sausage* (organic, starch-free only)	–	P		
Sirloin Steak (beef)	–	P		
Snails	–	P		
Snake	–	P		
Sweetbreads	–	P		
Tongue	–	P		
Tripe	–	P		
Turkey	–	P		
Veal	–	P		
Venison	–	P		
Wild Boar	–	P		
Witchetty Grubs	–	P		

FOOD	+/-/n	PROTEIN M/O	STARCH

Fish and Seafood (all acid-forming proteins) ∾

All fish and seafood are acid-forming proteins. Try to replace some meat meals with fresh fish when you can, but avoid those coated with batter or breadcrumbs. Fish will mix well with any non-starchy vegetables, salads, seeds and herbs but not with starchy vegetables, grains or cereals.

Abalone	−	P	
Anchovies	−	P	
Australian Bass	−	P	
Balmain Bug	−	P	
Barramundi	−	P	
Bass	−	P	
Blackfish	−	P	
Blue Grenadier	−	P	
Blue Threadfin	−	P	
Boarfish	−	P	
Bombay Duck	−	P	
Botargo	−	P	
Bream	−	P	
Brill	−	P	
Calamari (Squid)	−	P	
Carp	−	P	
Catfish	−	P	

FOOD	+/-/n	PROTEIN	M/O	STARCH
Caviar	–	P		
Chiton	–	P		
Clam	–	P		
Coalfish (Saithe)	–	P		
Cockles	–	P		
Cod	–	P		
Coley	–	P		
Conpoy	–	P		
Coral Trout	–	P		
Crab	–	P		
Crawfish	–	P		
Crayfish	–	P		
Cuttlefish	–	P		
Dab	–	P		
Dhu-Fish	–	P		
Dogfish	–	P		
Dover Sole	–	P		
Dried Shrimp (Ha Maai)	–	P		
Drummer	–	P		
Eel	–	P		
Emperor	–	P		
Flathead	–	P		
Flounder	–	P		
Freshwater Mussels	–	P		
Garfish	–	P		

FOOD	+/-/n	PROTEIN	M/O	STARCH
Gemfish	–	P		
Groper	–	P		
Gurnard	–	P		
Haddock	–	P		
Hairtail	–	P		
Hake	–	P		
Halibut	–	P		
Herring	–	P		
Hoke	–	P		
Hussar	–	P		
Ikan Bilis (dried)	–	P		
Jamaican Red Tilapia	–	P		
Jellyfish (edible)	–	P		
Jewfish (Mulloway)	–	P		
John Dory	–	P		
Kingfish	–	P		
Kipper	–	P		
Ku Rau	–	P		
Langoustine	–	P		
Leatherjacket	–	P		
Lemon Sole	–	P		
Ling	–	P		
Lobster	–	P		
Mackerel	–	P		
Megrim	–	P		

FOOD	+/-/n	PROTEIN	M/O	STARCH
Monkfish	–	P		
Moreton Bay Bug	–	P		
Mud Crab	–	P		
Mullet, Red and Grey	–	P		
Mulloway (Jewfish)	–	P		
Mussels	–	P		
Mussels, Freshwater	–	P		
Ocean Perch (Orange Roughy)	–	P		
Octopus	–	P		
Orange Roughy (Ocean Perch)	–	P		
Oysters	–	P		
Parrot Fish	–	P		
Pâté, Fish	–	P		
Perch	–	P		
Pike	–	P		
Pilchard	–	P		
Plaice	–	P		
Porgy	–	P		
Prawns	–	P		
Rainbow Trout	–	P		
Ray	–	P		
Redfish	–	P		
Rock Oysters	–	P		
Roe (all types)	–	P		
Saithe (Coalfish)	–	P		

FOOD	+/-/n	PROTEIN	M/O	STARCH
Salmon	–	P		
Salmon Trout	–	P		
Sardine	–	P		
Scallop	–	P		
Scampi (without breadcrumbs only)	–	P		
Sea Bream	–	P		
Sea Cucumber	–	P		
Sea Trout	–	P		
Sea Urchin	–	P		
Selar	–	P		
Shark	–	P		
Shrimps	–	P		
Skate	–	P		
Smoked Fish (any)*	–	P		
Smoked Salmon*	–	P		
Snapper	–	P		
Sole, Lemon and Dover	–	P		
Sprats	–	P		
Squid (Calamari)	–	P		
Swordfish	–	P		
Tailor	–	P		
Taramasalata	–	P		
Tasmanian Salmon	–	P		
Tenggiri	–	P		
Teraglin	–	P		

FOOD	+/-/n	PROTEIN	M/O	STARCH
Trevally	–	P		
Trout	–	P		
Trumpeter	–	P		
Tuna	–	P		
Turbot	–	P		
Whelks	–	P		
Whitebait	–	P		
White Pomfret	–	P		
Whiting	–	P		
Winkles	–	P		
Wrasse	–	P		
Yellowfin Tuna	–	P		

Eggs and Dairy Products ∾

Most foods in this protein list are acid-forming. Exceptions are live yoghurt, raw unpasteurized milk, buttermilk and whey which are all alkaline-forming and generally easier to digest. Eggs (acid-forming protein) should be truly free-range and not barn or battery raised. Cow's milk is best avoided or kept to an absolute minimum — see page 31 (and *Food Combining In 30 Days*) for further information.

Albumen (Egg White Protein)	–	P		
Bantam Eggs	–	P		

FOOD	+/-/n	PROTEIN	M/O	STARCH
Bio Yoghurt	+	P		
Buttermilk	+	P		
Cheeses (all types)	−	P		
Chicken's Eggs	−	P		
Condensed Milk	−	P		
Cow's Milk (see Milk)	−	P		
Dairy Ice Cream	−	P		
Duck Eggs	−	P		
Eggs, yolk *and* white (all types)	−	P		
Egg Replacer (see Soya)	−	P		
Emu Eggs	−	P		
Evaporated Milk	−	P		
Ewe's Milk (Sheep's Milk)	−	P		
Fromage Frais (additive free only)	+	P		
Goat's Milk	−	P		
Goat's Yoghurt	+	P		
Goose Eggs	−	P		
Greek Yoghurt	+	P		
Guinea Fowl Eggs	−	P		
Hen's Eggs	−	P		
Milk – Pasteurised*	−	P		
Milk – Unpasteurised*	+	P		
Ostrich Eggs		P		
Pheasant Eggs	−	P		
Powdered Milk		P		

FOOD	+/-/n	PROTEIN	M/O	STARCH
Preserved Duck Eggs (Pei Daan)	–	P		
Pullet Eggs	–	P		
Quail Eggs	–	P		
Salted Duck Eggs (Haam Daan)	–	P		
Seagull Eggs	–	P		
Semi-Skimmed Cow's Milk	–	P		
Sheep's Milk (Ewe's)	–	P		
Sheep's Yoghurt	+	P		
Skimmed Cow's Milk	–	P		
Smetana	–	P		
Turtle Eggs	–	P		
UHT Milk	–	P		
Whey	+	P		
Yoghurt	+	P		

Grains and Cereals ❧

Including breads, buns, crackers, biscuits, flour and pasta

Almost all grains and cereal products are acid-forming starches. They mix well with any kind of vegetables (starchy or non-starchy) and with salads, seeds and herbs but not, of course, with proteins. Remember that pasta should be egg-free; the protein from egg does not combine well with the starchy pasta flour.

FOOD	+/-/n	PROTEIN	M/O	STARCH
Anelini (must be egg-free)	−			S
Arborio Rice (Risotto Rice)	−			S
Arrowroot	+			S
Atta Flour	−			S
Bagel	−			S
Banana Flour	+			S
Bannocks	−			S
Bap	−			S
Barley	−			S
Barley Flour	−			S
Basmati Rice	−			S
Besan (Gram/Chickpea Flour)	−			S
Biscuits, Savoury	−			S
Biscuits, Sweet*	−			S
Black Rye (Pumpernickel)	−			S
Bread	−			S
Breadcrumbs	−			S
Breakfast Cereals	−			S
Brioche	−			S
Brown Bread	−			S
Brown Pasta (Wholemeal Pasta — must be egg-free)	−			S
Brown Rice	−			S
Buckwheat	−			S
Buckwheat Flour	−			S
Bulgar Wheat (Burghul/Cracked)	−			S

FOOD	+/-/n	PROTEIN	M/O	STARCH
Burghul Wheat (Bulgar/Cracked)	–			S
Calrose Rice	–			S
Chapati Flour	–			S
Chapatis	–			S
Chestnut Flour	–			S
Chickpea Flour (Besan/Gram Flour)	–			S
Ciabatta Bread	–			S
Conchigliette (must be egg-free)	–			S
Cookies*	–			S
Cornflour* (see Foods to Avoid)	–			S
Cornmeal	–			S
Couscous	–			S
Cracked Wheat (Bulgar/Burghul)	–			S
Crackers (Biscuits, Savoury)	–			S
Crispbread	–			S
Croissant	–			S
Crumpets	–			S
Custard Powder*	–			S
Damper	–			S
Danish Pastry	–			S
Diamantini (must be egg-free)	–			S
Ditalini (must be egg-free)	–			S
Doughnut	–			S
Dumplings	–			S
Durum Wheat	–			S

FOOD	+/-/n	PROTEIN M/O	STARCH
Farfalle (Bowtie Pasta — must be egg-free)	−		S
Farfallini (must be egg-free)	−		S
Flour (all types)	−		S
Focaccia (must be egg-free)	−		S
Fusilli (must be egg-free)	−		S
Gari (Cassava — dried)	−		S
Glutinous Rice			S
Gnocchetti (must be egg-free)	−		S
Gnocchi (must be egg-free)	−		S
Gramigna (must be egg-free)	−		S
Granary Bread	−		S
Green Pea Flour	−		S
Grissini (Bread Sticks)	−		S
Grits	−		S
Ground Rice	−		S
Hot Cross Bun	−		S
Italian Rice			S
Jasmine Rice (Thai Fragrant Rice)	−		S
Kamut			S
Kasha (Roasted Buckwheat)	−		S
Kuzu Powder	−		S
Lasagne (no protein filling)	−		S
Lavash	−		S
Lentil Flour	−		S
Linguine (must be egg-free)	−		S

FOOD	+/-/n	PROTEIN	M/O	STARCH
Long Grain Rice	−			S
Lotus Root Starch	−			S
Macaroni (must be egg-free)	−			S
Maize Flour	−			S
Maize Grits (Hominy)	−			S
Malt Flour	−			S
Matzo	−			S
Matzo Meal	−			S
Millet	+			S
Millet Flour	+			S
Muesli	−			S
Muffin	−			S
Naan	−			S
Noodles (must be egg-free)	−			S
Oat Biscuits	−			S
Oat Cakes	−			S
Oat Flour	−			S
Oatgerm	−			S
Oatmeal	−			S
Oats (rolled/porridge)	−			S
Orecchiette (must be egg-free)	−			S
Panettone	−			S
Pappadum	−			S
Paratha	−			S
Pasta (must be egg-free)	−			S
Pastry (all types)	−			S

FOOD	+/-/n	PROTEIN M/O	STARCH
Pearl Barley	–		S
Penne (must be egg-free)	–		S
Pitta	–		S
Pizza (base only)	–		S
Polenta	–		S
Popcorn	–		S
Porridge	–		S
Potato Flour	+		S
Pot Barley (Scotch Barley	–		S
Pretzels	–		S
Pumpernickel (Black Rye)	–		S
Puri	–		S
Quinoa	–		S
Red Rice	–		S
Rice (all types)	–		S
Rice Bran	–		S
Rice, Brown	–		S
Rice Cakes	–		S
Rice Flour	–		S
Rice, Long Grain	–		S
Rice Noodles	–		S
Rice, Short Grain	–		S
Rice, White	–		S
Risotto Rice (Arborio Rice)	–		S
Rissoni (must be egg-free)	–		S

FOOD	+/-/n	PROTEIN	M/O	STARCH
Rolls	–			S
Rye	–			S
Rye Bread	–			S
Rye Crispbread	–			S
Rye Flour	–			S
Sago	–			S
Salep Powder	–			S
Scotch Barley (Pot Barley)	–			S
Seitan (Zeitan)	–			S
Semolina				S
Short Grain Rice	–			S
Soda Bread	–			S
Sorghum	–			S
Sorghum Flour	–			S
Sourdough Bread	–			S
Spaghetti (must be egg-free)	–			S
Spelt	–			S
Springroll Wrapper	–			S
Tagliatelle (must be egg-free)	–			S
Tapioca	–			S
Taro Flour	+			S
Thai Fragrant Rice (Jasmine Rice)	–			S
Tortilla	–			S
Trenette (must be egg-free)	–			S
Triticale	–			S

FOOD	+/-/n	PROTEIN M/O	STARCH
Vermicelli (Capellini — must be egg-free)	–		S
Wheat	–		S
Wheat Noodles (must be egg-free)	–		S
Wheatgerm	–		S
White Bread	–		S
White Rice	–		S
Wholemeal Bread	–		S
Wholemeal Flour	–		S
Wholemeal Pasta (Brown Pasta — must be egg-free)	–		S
Wild Rice	–		S
Yam Flour	–		S
Zeitan (Seitan)	–		S

Fats and Oils
(mix with anything) ∿

Everything under this heading will combine with proteins or starches, all vegetables, herbs and salads. However, keep lard, dripping and suet to a minimum — or better still, avoid them altogether. They are acid-forming and are generally considered to be 'unhealthy' (see *The Food Combining Diet* for more information).

Almond Oil*	n	M
Apricot Kernel Oil*	n	M

FOOD	+/-/n	PROTEIN M/O	STARCH
Avocado Oil*	n	M	
Butter*	n	M	
Cocoa Butter*	n	M	
Coconut Milk*	n	M	
Coconut Oil*	n	M	
Cod Liver Oil	–	M	
Cold Pressed Oils*	n	M	
Corn Oil (Maize Oil)*	n	M	
Cottonseed Oil*	n	M	
Cream (cream is classed as fat not protein)*	n	M	
Crème Fraiche*	n	M	
Dripping*	–	M	
Extra Virgin Olive Oil*	n	M	
Flaxseed Oil (Linseed Oil)*	n	M	
Grapeseed Oil*	n	M	
Halibut Liver Oil*	–	M	
Hazelnut Oil*	n	M	
Lard*	–	M	
Linseed Oil (Flaxseed Oil)*	n	M	
Macadamia Oil*	n	M	
Maize Oil (Corn Oil)*	n	M	
Margarine (non hydrogenated only)*	n	M	
Mustard Oil*	n	M	
Palm Oil*	n	M	
Pecan Oil*	n	M	

FOOD	+/-/n	PROTEIN	M/O	STARCH
Polyunsaturated Spreads (non-hydrogenated only)*	n		M	
Pumpkin Seed Oil*	n		M	
Rapeseed Oil*	n		M	
Red Palm Oil*	n		M	
Ricebran Oil*	n		M	
Safflower Oil*	n		M	
Sesame Oil*	n		M	
Shortening*	–		M	
Soured Cream*	n		M	
Soyabean Oil*	n		M	
Suet*	–		M	
Sunflower Oil*	n		M	
Vanaspati (Vegetable Ghee)*	n		M	
Vegetable Ghee (Vanaspati)*	n		M	
Vegetable Oil*	n		M	
Walnut Oil*	n		M	
Wheatgerm Oil*	n		M	

Pulses (Legumes) (all acid-forming) ∾

Under food combining law, pulses are a 'special case'. Turn to page 25 for more information.

Adzuki Bean (Aduki)*	–			
Baked Beans*	–			

FOOD	+/-/n	PROTEIN	M/O	STARCH
Black Bean (Dow See/Salted Black Bean): see soya list*	+	P		
Black Kidney Bean (Turtle Bean)*	−			
Black-Eyed Bean/Pea (Cowpea/Catjang)*	−			
Blue Pea (Whole Dried Pea)*	−			
Borlotti Bean (Roman Bean/Pink Bean)*	−			
Broad Bean − Dried (Fava Bean)*	−			
Brown Bean*	−			
Brown Lentils*	−			
Butter Bean (Lima Bean)*	−			
Cannellini Bean (Great Northern Bean)*	−			
Catjang (Black-Eyed Bean/Black-Eyed Pea/Cowpea)*	−			
Chickpea (Garbanzo Bean)*	−			
Continental Lentils (Green Lentils)*	−			
Cowpea (Black-Eyed Bean/Black-Eyed Pea/Catjang)*	−			
Egyptian Brown Bean (Ful Medami)*	−			
Falafel*	−			
Fava Bean (Broad Bean − dried)*	−			
Flageolet Bean*	−			
Ful Medami (Egyptian Brown Bean)*	−			
Garbanzo Bean (Chickpea)*	−			
Great Northern Bean (Cannellini Bean)*	−			
Green Gram (Mung Bean/Moong Dal)*	−			

FOOD	+/-/n	PROTEIN	M/O	STARCH
Green Lentils (Continental Lentils)*	-			
Haricot Bean (Navy Bean)*	-			
Hummus (made from chick peas)*	-			
Hyacinth Bean (Lablab)*	-			
Kidney Bean*	-			
Lablab (Hyacinth Bean)*	-			
Lentils (all types)*	-			
Lima Bean (Butter Bean)*	-			
Lupin Bean*	-			
Marrowfat Peas*	-			
Moong Dal (Mung Bean/Green Gram)*	-			
Mung Bean (Green Gram/Moong Dal)*	-			
Mungbean Vermicelli (Fun See)*	-			
Mushy Peas*	-			
Navy Bean (Haricot Bean)*	-			
Peanut (Groundnut)* (organic only)	-			
Peanut Butter* (organic only)	-			
Pease Pudding*	-			
Pigeon Pea*	-			
Pink Bean (Borlotti Bean/Roman Bean)*	-			
Pinto Bean*	-			
Raajma (Red Kidney Bean)*	-			
Red Kidney Bean (Raajma)*	-			
Red Lentils (Split Lentils)*	-			
Roman Bean (Borlotti Bean)*	-			

FOOD	+/-/n	PROTEIN	M/O	STARCH
Rose Coco Bean*	−			
Split Peas*	−			
Turtle Bean (Black Kidney Bean)*	−			
Whole Dried Pea (Blue Pea)*	−			

Soya Protein ∾

Soya and soya products should be treated as protein
foods and are not suitable for mixing with starches. See
page 26 for more information about soya products.

Beancurd (Tofu/Dau Foo)*	+	P		
Black Soya Bean (Salted Black Bean/Dow See)*	+	P		
Dow See (Black Soya Bean/Salted Black Bean)*	−	P		
Egg Replacer*	−	P		
Hatcho Miso*	−	P		
Miso*	−	P		
Mugi Miso*	−	P		
Okara (Soya Fibre)*	−	P		
Soya Beans*	−	P		
Soya Cheese*	−	P		
Soya Cream*	−	P		
Soya Drink (Soya Milk)*	−	P		
Soya Flour*	−	P		

FOOD	FAMILY	+/-/n	PROTEIN	M/O	STARCH
Soya Ice Cream*		–	P		
Soya Lecithin*		–	P		
Soya Yoghurt*		–	P		
Tempeh*		–	P		
Tofu (Beancurd/Dau Foo)*		–	P		
TVP – Textured Vegetable Protein*		–	P		

Starchy Vegetables (all alkaline-forming) ↝

These vegetables are distinct from non–starchy vegetables in that they contain a high *proportion* of starch.
This means that they don't combine comfortably with
protein foods. However, they are all healthily alkaline-
forming and very versatile. Mix starchy vegetables with
salads, herbs, seeds and (in moderation) with other
starches.

Batata (Faan Sue/Sweet Potato)		+			S
Breadfruit		+			S
Bush Potato		+			S
Cassava (Manioc)		+			S
Cheeky Yam		+			S
Chips (shallow-fried in olive oil only)		+			S
Colocasi		+			S
Corn on the Cob		+			S

FOOD	FAMILY	+/-/n	PROTEIN	M/O	STARCH
Cycad	+				S
Dasheen (Eddoes/Taro/Kandalla)	+				S
Eddoes (Taro/Dasheen/Kandalla)	+				S
Flat Swamp Potato	+				S
Flax Lily	+				S
Grass Potato	+				S
Kalumburu Yam	+				S
Kandalla (Eddoes/Taro/Dasheen)	+				S
King Orchid	+				S
Kudzu Root (Fun Got)	+				S
Kumara Sweet Potato	+				S
Long Yam	+				S
Maize (Corn)	+				S
Malanga	+				S
Manioc (Cassava)	+				S
Matoki	+				S
Melokhia (Jew's Mallow)	+				S
Pencil Yam	+				S
Potato	+				S
Potato Orchid	+				S
Red Sweet Potato	+				S
Spike Rush	+				S
Sweet Potato (Faan Sue)	+				S
Sweetcorn	+				S
Tannia	+				S

FOOD	FAMILY	+/-/n	PROTEIN	M/O	STARCH
Taro (Eddoes/Dasheen/Kandalla)	+				S
White Sweet Potato	+				S
Yam (Shu Yu)	+				S
Yam Bean (Jicama/Sha Ge)	+				S

Condiments, Flavourings and Seasonings ❧

Ideally, the items in the following list should never be used in excess; indeed they are usually only added to foods in very small amounts. Such relatively minute quantities are unlikely to disturb digestive function or affect food combinations. For this reason, there is no need to worry about the classification of condiments, flavourings or seasonings shown here. For the purposes of food combining, treat them all as 'mix-with-anything' items but keep them to a minimum.

White Pepper

Black Pepper

Peppercorns

Salt

Celery Salt

Garlic Salt

Rock Salt

Sea Salt

Potassium Salt

Salt Substitutes

Sesame Salt (Gomasio)

Worcestershire Sauce

Oyster Sauce (Ho yau)

Chutney/Pickle

Mayonnaise/Salad Cream (both egg-based so, strictly speaking, better *not* mixed with starch foods)

Cider Vinegar

Wine Vinegar

Essences and Natural Flavourings (e.g. Vanilla)

Light Soy Sauce (See yau)
Dark Soy Sauce (Lo chau)

Alcohol ❧

People always want to know where alcohol fits in to the food combining scenario! Alcohol is, in fact, made from food substances but, once produced, could more properly be called a beverage. The Hay school of thought says that grain-based drinks (e.g. beer) should be taken only with starch meals and that fruit-based wines, ciders etc. with protein. But this can become tortuous and is, in my view, unnecessary. How many people, for example, drink alcohol at every meal?

Large amounts of any kind of alcohol can adversely affect the appetite and upset the digestion too — so moderation is obviously important. Studies show that a small daily intake of good-quality wine can be very good for us. My experience with patients is that wine seems to combine comfortably with protein or starch meals but that beer is best kept to a minimum and not taken in large amounts with food. A small measure of spirit or fortified wine as an aperitif can be beneficial and is a pleasant social activity.

In other words, drink moderately and sensibly and don't worry about how you combine it.

Beverages ∾

Small amounts of coffee and tea do not appear to cause any food combining catastrophes and it really isn't necessary to worry about how to combine them. Those of good quality can be therapeutic and enjoyable in small quantities. However, when taken in large amounts (especially near to mealtimes), they may upset the absorption of some vitamins and minerals. It's wiser, then, to drink your favourite beverages in moderation and between meals, rather than with food. And there's a wonderful selection of herb teas available nowadays — so why not experiment with these?

Cola and other canned 'fizz' may be popular but, from a healthy eating/drinking perspective are really best avoided or taken only occasionally.

Added Sweetenings ∾

Sugar and sugary foods are, quite literally, a 'sticky' food combining area. Some experts believe that sugars (being basically carbohydrates) should fall under the same heading as starches and this is where I have always listed them. Other writers have expressed concern at such a combination and say that sugars don't mix well with anything. If we follow common-sense, then it is likely that we will use sugars and syrups in such small amounts that the actual combinations become relatively unimportant. Clinical experience with my own patients suggests that small quantities of unrefined, natural sugar (i.e. blackstrap molasses or that found in fresh fruits and cold-pressed honey) do not present any food combining dilemma, nor do they appear to interfere with the digestion of other foods. Large amounts, however, have the potential to disturb the delicate balance of blood glucose, to aggravate thrush or candidiasis and also to use up or destroy valuable nutrients in the system.

My modified rule is, therefore, that sugars and sugary foods can be enjoyed in small amounts, but should otherwise be avoided wherever possible. Brown sugars are, sorry to report, no healthier than the ordinary pure, white and deadly stuff! Where sweetenings are required, cold-pressed honey or molasses are likely to be better options. Carob Bars, Carob Spread and Carob Powder can be included here as they usually contain sugar. However, use small amounts only.

So, where extra sweetness is needed, choose from the following list and keep to small quantities:

Honey – cold-pressed only

Blackstrap molasses

Fruit sugar (fructose)

Maple syrup (real, natural only)

Crystallized ginger

Barbados sugar

Carob bar

Carob spread

Desserts, Puddings and Sugary Foods ∾

There are spoilsports who believe that we should desert
desserts entirely. It is true that the majority of desserts
and puddings are poor protein/starch combinations,
containing flour, egg, milk and/or fruit in varying
quantities as well as lots of unhealthy sugar. For this
reason, they are not recommended for serious food
combiners and so do not appear in the food lists.
However, the occasional treat is unlikely to be harmful
and should be enjoyed thoroughly!

Quick Reference Chart

You can mix the *Proteins* in **COLUMN A**
with anything from **COLUMN B**

or mix the *Starches* in **COLUMN C**
with anything from **COLUMN B**

but don't mix **COLUMN A** with **COLUMN C**.

COLUMN A PROTEINS 'P'	COLUMN B MIX WITH ANYTHING 'M'	COLUMN C STARCHES 'S'
Fish (page 136)	Non-starchy vegetables (page 115)	Starchy vegetables (page 156)
Shellfish (page 136)	All salads (page 115)	Grains & Cereals (page 144)
Eggs & Dairy (page 142)	Herbs & Spices (page 125)	Noodles & Pasta (page 144)
Meat, Poultry & Game (page 134)	Nuts (page 132)	Bread, Biscuits & Pastry (page 144)
Soya beans & all soya products (page 155)	Seeds (page 130)	
	Fats & Oils (page 151)	
	Condiments, Flavourings & Seasonings (page 158)	

Important notes:

- You will see that fruits and fruit juices do not appear in the quick reference list (above). Page 20 explains why they do not mix well with other foods.
- Pulses are not included here since they are treated as a 'special case'. This does not, however, mean that they are to be avoided. They mix well with salads and vegetables and in moderation with starches but never well with proteins. See page 25 for more information on pulses and how to include them and page 155 for a full list of choices.
- Nuts are a very concentrated food and some people find them difficult to digest. They can be mixed in moderation with other foods but, if they cause you discomfort, try them with vegetables or salad foods only and not with proteins or starches. A full list can be found on page 134. It is worth remembering that peanuts are not nuts but pulses and can be a common allergen. If you're a peanut butter fan, try the organic version from your health food store.

Sources of Reference

❧

The Encyclopaedia of Food and Nutrition. Jo Rogers, Merehurst 1990.

A Guide To Common Vegetables. Ed: Joyce T.S. Foo, Singapore Science Centre 1991.

The Composition of Foods (Fifth Edition). McCance & Widdowson, Royal Society of Chemistry 1992.

Fruit and Nuts. First Supplement to McCance & Widdowson's *The Composition of Foods* (Fourth Edition). Royal Society of Chemistry 1992.

Cereals and Cereal Products. Third Supplement to McCance & Widdowson's *The Composition of Foods* (Fourth Edition). Royal Society of Chemistry 1988.

Milk Products and Eggs. Fourth Supplement to McCance & Widdowson's *The Composition of Foods* (Fourth Edition). Royal Society of Chemistry 1989.

Vegetables Herbs and Spices. Fifth Supplement to McCance & Widdowson's *The Composition of Foods* (Fourth Edition). Royal Society of Chemistry 1991.

Table of Composition of Australia Aboriginal Foods. Janette Brand Miller, Keith W. James, Patricia M.A. Maggiore, Aboriginal Studies Press 1993.

Manual of Nutrition Eighth Edition. Ed: David Buss and

Jean Robertson, Ministry of Agriculture, Fisheries and Food 1984, Her Majesty's Stationery Office.

Dietary Reference Values for Food Energy and Nutrients for the United Kingdom. Report of the Panel on Dietary Reference Values of the Committee on Medical Aspects of Food Policy, Department of Health 1991, Her Majesty's Stationery Office.

Food and Healing. Annemarie Colbin, Ballantine Books, New York 1986.

Fit For Life. Harvey and Marilyn Diamond, Bantam Books 1987.

Eating Alive. Dr Jonn Matsen, Crompton Books 1987.

Food Combining Made Easy. Dr Herbert M. Shelton, Willow Publishing Inc. 1982.

Immigrant Foods. Second supplement to McCance & Widdowson's *The Composition of Foods.* Ministry of Agriculture, Fisheries and Food 1985, Her Majesty's Stationery Office.

A Popular Guide To Chinese Vegetables. Karen Phillipps and Martha Dahlen, Frederick Muller Ltd 1983.

Food and Nutrition, Customs and Culture. Paul Fieldhouse, Chapman and Hall 1991.

Nutrition (Ninth Edition). Margaret S. Chaney, Margaret L. Ross and Jelia C. Witschi, Houghton Mifflin Company, Boston 1979.

The California Nutrition Book. Paul Saltman PhD, Joel Gurin and Ira Mothner, Little, Brown & Company 1987.

A Doctor in the Wilderness. Dr Walter Yellowlees, Janus Publishing 1993.

The Composition of Foods, Milk Products & Eggs (Fourth Edition). McCance & Widdowson, B. Holland, I.D. Unwin and D.H. Buss. Royal Society of Chemistry/

Ministry of Agriculture, Fisheries & Food. 1989.
Food Portion Sizes. Helen Crawley. Ministry of
Agriculture, Fisheries & Food, HMSO, 1990.

My thanks also to Malmesbury Library for their help
with the research for *The Food Combiner's Meal Planner*.

Food Families Index

By the same author:

FOOD COMBINING IN 30 DAYS

Kathryn Marsden

Everyone is talking about food combining — also known as The Hay Diet. In *Food Combining in 30 Days*, leading nutritionist Kathryn Marsden has created a health plan that really works.

Easy to follow, taking one day at a time, this book explains clearly how food combining works — for weight loss, and improving health and vitality. It includes:

- a step by step approach to the food combining rules
- easy recipe ideas divided into starch, protein and alkaline meals
- revitalizing exercises
- health tips for an improved lifestyle

After a week you'll be feeling better than ever before. By the end of day 30 you'll be feeling fit for life.

THE FOOD COMBINING DIET

Kathryn Marsden

- No counting calories
- No small portions
- Few forbidden foods

The Food Combining Diet is the easy, flexible, healthy way to lose weight. Leading nutritionist Kathryn Marsden has devised four weeks of easy recipes which include 3 meals a day, already divided into the three food categories of starch, protein, and alkaline meals.

The recipes can either be followed strictly day by day or mixed and matched by more confident food combiners.

There are useful health tips and simple explanations as well as ideas for menu planning.

This is not a 'quick fix' diet. Based on the Hay system of food combining, this carefully devised eating plan allows you to enjoy your food while you lose weight — safely.

Nothing could be simpler. *The Food Combining Diet* is the perfect introduction to a new way of eating for life.

Explains so simply how to adopt food combining. Tremendous.' *Katie Boyle*

FOOD COMBINING FOR VEGETARIANS

Jackie Le Tissier

What is food combining? A wonderful way of eating for health which can be adapted for life. Simply by separating starch from protein and increasing the quantity of alkaline foods in your daily diet you can work with your body to lose weight, increase your health and vitality, and improve your resistance to illness.

Jackie Le Tissier has been vegetarian food combining for years. Her inspiring recipes will show you how to put the diet into practice.

Discover:

- Delicious recipes for every occasion
- Which foods to eat and which to avoid
- Original menus and serving suggestions

and much much more!

'A book that all food combiners will enjoy, not just vegetarians.' *Doris Grant*

FOOD COMBINING FOR HEALTH

Doris Grant and Jean Joice

Food Combining for Health is the international bestseller that has improved the health and vitality of thousands.

Also known as *The Hay Diet*, it is based on Dr William Howard Hay's eating system, devised nearly 100 years ago. Simply by keeping starch foods separate from protein foods in your daily diet, foods can be digested more easily, and your general health improved.

Many have found it has helped to alleviate:

- Arthritic pain
- Digestive disorders
- Ulcers
- Obesity

and many other health problems.

Doris Grant and Jean Joice have taken a fresh look at Dr Hay's teachings. They offer lots of practical advice and suggestions including a comprehensive recipe section to show you how easy it can be to begin food combining for life.

THE FOOD COMBINING DIET	0 7225 2790 X	£4.99	☐
FOOD COMBINING IN 30 DAYS	0 7225 2960 0	£4.99	☐
FOOD COMBINING FOR VEGETARIANS	0 7225 2763 2	£4.99	☐
FOOD COMBINING FOR HEALTH	0 7225 2506 0	£4.99	☐

All these books are available from your local bookseller or can be ordered direct from the publishers.

To order direct just tick the titles you want and fill in the form below:

Name: _____

Address: _____

_____

_____ Postcode:_____

Send to: Thorsons Mail Order, Dept 3, HarperCollins*Publishers*, Westerhill Road, Bishopbriggs, Glasgow G64 2QT.
Please enclose a cheque or postal order or your authority to debit your Visa/Access account —

Credit card no: _____

Expiry date: _____

Signature: _____

— up to the value of the cover price plus:
UK & BFPO: Add £1.00 for the first book and 25p for each additional book ordered.
Overseas orders including Eire: Please add £2.95 service charge. Books will be sent by surface mail but quotes for airmail despatches will be given on request.

24 HOUR TELEPHONE ORDERING SERVICE FOR ACCESS/VISA CARDHOLDERS — TEL.: 0141 772 2281